Succeed in
English

A comprehensive guide to a clearer understanding
of reading, writing and grammar.

Key Stage 3
Ages 11–14

Katharine Watson

Consultant: Martin Manser

INDEX

This edition published 2002
for Index Books Limited
Henson Way, Kettering, Northamptonshire NN16 8PX

Copyright © Arcturus Publishing Limited
1-7 Shand Street, London SE1 2ES

ISBN 1-84193-094-6

Printed and bound in Italy

Author: Katharine Watson
Editor: Paula Field
Consultant Editor: Martin Manser
Designer: Zeta Fitzpatrick @ Moo Design
Cover designer: Alex Ingr

CONTENTS

INTRODUCTION

During this part of your time at school you **discover how to write** for a whole range of purposes.

• You begin to **develop a personal style of writing** which is attractive and pleasing to the reader.

• You learn to **present thoughts, ideas and information** clearly and logically.

• As you understand more and more how words and language work, you discover how to **produce writing that is interesting, lively and original**.

The kind of writing you will need to do in English falls into four broad categories.

CREATIVE WRITING

This is where you use your imagination to delight your reader, creating stories, poems or plays out of your own head.

INFORMATIVE WRITING

Here you learn to find, select and present facts and information in a lively and interesting way in articles, reports, leaflets etc.

PERSUASIVE WRITING

*The purpose of this kind of writing is to persuade your readers to accept a particular point of view, putting the case **for** something or **against** something. You learn how to present a logical argument. (Note: look up the word 'argument' in your dictionary. It has more than one meaning.)*

REFLECTIVE OR ANALYTICAL WRITING

This kind of writing is for thinking. You may be asked to reflect on your own experiences and feelings, and write about them. Or you might think about something someone else has said or written, and comment on it. You will also need to learn how to analyse poems, plays and stories, and write detailed commentaries on them.

In this section you will find instructions and hints on how to tackle all these different kinds of writing. There are also exercises for you to practise for yourself.

Writing is a wonderful way to discover what you actually think about things. It helps you sort your thoughts out and also find out how much you really know. It's also great fun and brilliantly satisfying.

So enjoy it!

INTRODUCTION

Some people say it's impossible to teach a person to write; they either have a talent for it, or they don't. It is true that some people are naturally talented as writers, because they have an 'ear' for the sound and rhythm of language, just as a musical person has an 'ear' for music. But anyone, so long as he or she follows these few simple principles, can become, if not a brilliant writer, at least a very good one.

BEFORE YOU START, LISTEN

Wait for the words to come to you. Be patient. Don't try to force anything. When you can hear the first sentence, write it down.

FIND THE RIGHT WORD

Be sure you have exactly the right word for the job. That means it must carry the precise meaning you want, and it must sound right in your sentence. Don't be satisfied with just any old word. Always treat words with respect. If you're not quite happy with a word, try using your thesaurus to see if you can find a better one.

SIMPLE IS BEAUTIFUL

Aim to write simply and clearly. On the whole, it is better to not to use a long word when a short one will do the job just as well.

NO UNNECESSARY WORDS

If you don't really need a word, cross it out. (For example, the word 'very' is almost always unnecessary. It doesn't really add anything, and it takes away from the force of what you are saying.) Be strict with yourself about this.

BE BRIEF

Put what you have to say in as few words as possible. Try out different ways of expressing it until you find the neatest and most satisfying one.

BE GENEROUS

Write fully. Don't hold back. Think carefully whether you have covered all appropriate aspects of what you are writing about.

VARY YOUR SENTENCE STRUCTURE

If you have written several long, involved sentences, follow them with a short snappy one. If your writing tends to consist of a series of short, jerky little sentences, practise writing longer ones using subordinate clauses.

BE LOGICAL

Divide your material into topics, with a separate paragraph for each one.

GET THE FLOW

Link your paragraphs so that each one follows on smoothly and logically from the last one, and your reader can easily follow the train of your thought.

LISTEN

Listen to every word. Only by listening can you judge whether what you are writing is 'just right' or not. Listen to each sentence. Hear the whole sentence. Hear how it sounds in relation to the next sentence. Listen to each paragraph – to its beginning and ending. Listen to your piece as a whole. Hear it to the very last full stop.

INTRODUCTION

Let's begin with the most basic kind of writing – the sort of thing you probably get asked to do quite a lot – **writing about personal experiences**. How often have you been given a title like 'My visit to the zoo', or 'What I did in the holidays' to write about in English? Oh dear, how boring.

But it needn't be boring – not if you give it a little thought. The key is to think which were the really interesting or unusual bits, and write about them.

WHERE TO START?

If you shut your eyes and go back to the time of the experience itself – what stands out? What picture comes to your mind? You could start there. Suppose, for instance, on your zoo visit, you particularly liked the elephants. You might start your piece something like this:

> 'There is something about elephants. I'm not sure exactly what it is. Maybe it's because they are so big, and so wrinkly. Or perhaps it's the way they look so wise. Or the fact that they have been around on this earth for such a very long time. Whatever it is, somehow you can't help liking an elephant…'

And then you go on to write about the particular elephant you saw.

Another way to start might be to say how much you REALLY didn't want to go on that trip – and then explain how in the end it turned out much better than you expected.

Or you might begin by describing a moment, or an incident that happened, during the course of your visit:

> 'Suddenly the lion roared. It was an extraordinary sound, like nothing I had ever heard before. For a moment, everyone fell respectfully silent. The king of the jungle had spoken…'

GRABBING YOUR READER'S ATTENTION

In any piece of writing, you should always aim from the very first sentence to get your reader hooked. Try to think of a striking or unusual way to begin. You can slip in the more ordinary details later. But you should never begin your piece with the kind of routine 'We went to the station and we got on the train' introduction that teachers unfortunately have to plough through all too often. After all what else would you do at a station? Now if you had written, 'We went to the station and there was an earthquake,' that would be something.

> **LEAVE OUT THE DULL STUFF**
> Nobody really needs to know how you got to the zoo, or wherever it was. We don't need to know what time you arrived, or what you ate for lunch either. Leave out all that kind of thing. Concentrate on what matters. Similarly, if what you did in the holidays was visit your aunt and uncle in Delhi or New York, we don't want to read all about how long you spent at the airport and how you fastened your seatbelt. Tell us about the place! (Of course, if you travelled by hot air balloon or on the back of a camel, that would be a different matter.)

SO WHAT SHOULD YOU WRITE ABOUT?

Tell us about the sights, the sounds, the smells, the people you met, the things you did. Bring it all alive for us. Remember – we haven't been there. Your own experience, no matter how seemingly ordinary, is unique. We want to know about it. Another thing: tell us about your own reactions. What were your thoughts and feelings? Looking back, what do you feel about it now?

DOING NOTHING IS VERY NEARLY IMPOSSIBLE

'What did you do in the holidays/at half term?'
'Nothing.'
How often have you heard that little exchange? Perhaps you have even given the answer 'nothing' yourself. Well, it's not true that you did nothing. Go on, try it. Do nothing for five minutes. You must not move, hear anything, see anything, think anything, feel anything for five whole minutes. Try it now…

Not possible, is it? Even if you only sat watching television most of the time, you could write about the room you sat in, the other people who share it with you, the way the light slants in through the window… You could write about the thoughts that went through your mind, what made you choose one programme over another. Or the noises in the street outside, or the spider that crawled across the floor. All you need do is wake up a little, and there's a whole world, right under your nose. And it's waiting for you to write about it.

FOR PRACTICE

1. Challenge yourself: write a really lively account of one of these:

      a. A visit to a friend's house
      b. Going to the local park
      c. A day by yourself at home.

2. Think back over your life so far. What occasion stands out most vividly in your memory? Write about it.

3. What is the most exciting and memorable trip you have ever been on? Write about that. (Remember – leave out the dull bits.)

4. Write a piece called 'My Favourite Place'. Bring it really alive. Make your reader feel he or she is really there, seeing it with you.

WRITING A STORY

INTRODUCTION

So you have been asked to write a story. How are you to set about it? Where do you get ideas from? How do you put your ideas together into the right kind of shape to make a story that works?

GENRE

There are many different kinds of story. Here are some of them. Perhaps you can think of more:

- Adventure stories • Fantasy or mystery stories
- Crime or murder stories • War stories
- Science fiction stories, or stories about the future
- Stories about ships and the sea
- Historical stories about the lives of people in the past
- Stories about families, friendships, or relationships
- Stories about growing up • Animal stories
- Love stories • Funny stories

We call these different types of story different GENRES. ('Genre' is a French word; it means 'kind' or 'type'.)

WRITING TO SUIT YOUR CHOSEN GENRE

One of the first things you have to decide is what genre of story you are going to write. This will affect what style you write in, and what kinds of things can sensibly happen in your story. For example, if you are writing about two friends at school, and what happens when a new pupil arrives in their class, you wouldn't want suddenly to introduce monsters, or spaceships, or aliens, or a murder. (In fact, it is best to avoid monsters, aliens and murders altogether, unless you have been asked to write that kind of story. It is very difficult to write fantasy, science fiction or crime writing well unless you have had a lot of practice at other kinds of writing first.)

DO AS THE PROFESSIONALS DO

If you open any book and read the first page or so, you should be able to tell at once what kind of story it is – what **genre** the author has chosen. And you'll find that authors always stick to the same genre throughout the book; they know that nothing else works.

FOR PRACTICE
Make a list of up to ten books you, your friends or your parents have read recently, and decide to which **genre** each one belongs.

THE MAIN CHARACTER OR PROTAGONIST

Almost all stories have a central character, or hero. This could be a man, a woman, a boy, a girl, a dog, a horse, an angel, a ghost – or even, as in some children's stories, a car or a train.

The main character is the person that we *identify* with – the person we are most interested in, and care about and sympathise with. We want to know what happens to that person, what they are thinking, what they are feeling. If they are in trouble or danger, we want them to be saved. If they are frightened, we feel fear too.

WHO IS YOUR MAIN CHARACTER?

So one of your first decisions will be – who is your main character? In some stories – for example about friends sharing a holiday adventure – there may be two main characters, both equally important, or sometimes, in a longer novel, a whole group. But in a short story you will not have time to develop more than two main characters convincingly.

FOR PRACTICE

1. Write a list of ten books you have read, or, if you like, films you have seen. Who was the main character in each of them? Which was the character that the writer or director intended us, the readers or audience, to identify with? Was there just one main character, or more than one?

2. Imagine you are going to write two stories, each in a different genre. For each story, decide who is to be the main character. Think about them, imagine them as if they were real. Try to see them, hear their voices, think what kind of people they are. Do you like them? Do other people like them? What about their families, their friends, their homes, the things they like doing? When you have had a good think, spend five minutes writing detailed notes about each of them.

WHO ARE THEY?
Don't just write a lsit of characteristics off the top of your head – *really* see the person. Find out who they are.

THE NARRATOR

Your next major decision will be, who is going to tell this story? Who it the **narrator**, or storyteller? Is it going to be one of the characters in the story? If so, it may be the main character, or another character. Here are two examples to give you the idea.

> **A.** When I was young, I used to be very afraid of the dark. Little did I dream, then, that I would have to spend several days trapped underground, alone and terrified, in a disused mineshaft. It all began one summer's day last year. I was hiking across the Yorkshire moors with a couple of old friends from school days. We had been walking for about two hours, when suddenly...

> **B.** Josh Pickford was an unusual sort of boy. I was drawn to him, somehow, from the beginning. The first time I saw him, he was standing in the middle of a crowd of boys in the school playground. There had been a fight, and I noticed the calm way he quietly sorted the quarrel out and then seemed almost to disappear. He was always like that – cool. But I didn't really get to know him properly until...

NARRATIVE POINT OF VIEW

In story A, the 'I' of the story is both narrator (teller) and its hero. In story B, Josh Pickford is the hero, but the narrator is another boy telling us about him. There is a difference in **narrative point of view**.

FIRST OR THIRD PERSON NARRATIVE?

Another way of telling a story is to have the narrator as an unseen voice outside the story altogether. The narrator tells us what happens in the story without being a part of it. In the next extract, story C, the main character is Jenny, and we, the readers, are able to watch her – her thoughts and actions – from the point of view of a spectator outside the story.

> **C.** As Jenny lay in her narrow little bed in the attic she shivered – whether from fear or from cold she was not sure. Through the wooden floor she could hear voices raised in anger. Earlier, the clatter of horses' hooves and the sound of carriage wheels on the road in front of the inn had told her that some, at least, of the men who had been drinking below were going home. But still her father did not come upstairs to his room, and still the voices rose and fell. She wondered if the stranger who spoke with a foreign accent was among them. She had not liked the look of him.

We call the way of telling stories A and B, where the narrator is 'I', **first person narrative**. Where there is no 'I', but the narrator is a detached external observer, we call this **third person narrative**. (In grammar, we refer to 'I' and 'we' as First Person, 'you' as Second Person, and 'he', 'she', 'it' or 'they' as Third Person.)

FOR PRACTICE

1. Continue each of stories A, B and C for a few more lines, making sure that what you write fits the story so far.

2. Write the opening paragraph of the two stories, but with a different narrative point of view – once as a first person narrative, and once as a third person narrative.

THE SETTING

Your story will be set in a particular time and place – or series of times and places. It is up to you to make the place and the time seem real. You need not necessarily describe the various settings directly (although you may of course want to), but you should always see them in your own mind, and make them clear for your reader by the use of careful little details.

In the three examples we have had so far, story A is set on the Yorkshire moors (and later, presumably, down a mineshaft) in summer, in more or less the present time. (The story refers to events that happened 'last year'.) Story B is set in the environment of school. It could be present day, or possibly earlier this century. There are no details yet to fix it at a particular time.

Story C is set in an inn and the mention of horses and a carriage tells us at once that the story takes place in a past century. (Also note that, if it had been set in the present day, the narrator would have said 'pub' rather than 'inn'.)

CREATE A REALISTIC SETTING

Here are a couple of examples to help you get the idea of how to create a realistic setting. Of course you should always try to 'see' it in your mind's eye first, before you write about it. (Story-writing is not, as you have probably gathered by now, about 'making things up' – it's about seeing or *visualising* things in your mind, and then describing what you see.)

D. Tom sat down, panting, beside the little stream. After a while he began to relax. The grass felt warm in the afternoon sun, and it was pleasant to listen to the sound of the water chuckling over the smooth pebbles. Tom threw a small twig into the stream and watched it plunge over a tiny waterfall and then become stuck, circling round and round in a small eddy on the other side of the stream. Should he just stay here, he wondered, and let his pursuers come and take him?

E. Mr Bolsover led the way down the steps, shining his torch into dusty corners of the cellar as he went. I followed him cautiously, uncertain of what I might find myself treading upon. In addition to the musty, damp smell of mildew, there was a faint, sweetish, rather sickly smell that I could not quite identify. As the torch beams sought out various piles of what looked like rubbish, I could make out a lot of electric wiring, most of it covered in dust and spiders' webs. Suddenly, out of the darkness a gleam caught my eye.

Notice that the 'ingredients' which make up the setting and atmosphere are the senses: sights, sounds, smells, touch and even taste; the weather and the quality of light; the time of day; and whether the event is taking place indoors or outdoors.

> **FOR PRACTICE**
> Write a paragraph or two from the middle of two very different stories, creating a clear setting and atmosphere in both.

OTHER CHARACTERS

As well as your main character, there will probably be one or two other significant characters. You will need to make them real through description too.

Remember that the important part about a character is not so much what he or she looks like or is wearing (though that may be a necessary part of your description), but what his or her character and inner qualities are like. We want to know what kind of thing your characters think, feel, say – what kind of intentions they may have – and whether we are supposed to like them, dislike them, or perhaps fear them.

WHOSE SIDE ARE WE ON?

Your main character will probably be someone we like (otherwise we won't be on his or her side). In Story B, we are obviously meant to like Josh Pickford, and we learn a little about his character in the first few sentences. But there will also be unpleasant characters. The man in the bar in Story C is meant to be a little sinister. We can guess straight away that he will turn out to be the villain (the "baddie") of the story. Mr Bolsover in Story E could go either way – we can't tell, but we can probably guess that there is going to be something a bit worrying in that cellar. Mr Bolsover may or may not have a hand in it.

BUILD YOUR CHARACTERS

Characters are built up gradually in a story from: what they look like, how they dress, what kind of facial expressions they have, how they talk, what they say, what they do. What they do is probably the least important factor in creating your characters. In most stories, characters are given a paragraph of description (by way of an introduction to us), when they first appear in the story. (You could check that out by looking at one or two books you have read recently.)

You need not treat all your characters in the same detail. Some will only have minor parts, and need only brief and sketchy details. (These, incidentally, are called **secondary characters**.)

IT DOESN'T HAVE TO BE HUMAN!

Occasionally, you will come across a story where something other than a person is in effect a 'character' in the tale. For example, in a story set in the Arctic Circle, it might be the cold itself; or in South America, the jungle, closing in on its victims; or in a story set on board a ship, the sea. *The Old Man and the Sea* by Ernest Hemingway is such a story.

> **UNNECESSARY CHARACTERS**
> Don't put unnecessary characters into your story. You will have a hard enough time keeping alive the ones you do need, without adding extra ones.

> **FOR PRACTICE**
> Write two or three paragraphs, which could be from the same story or from different ones, in which you introduce a new character into the story. See how much information you can convey about each one of these new characters through your choice of details.

DIALOGUE

Your characters will speak to each other! In fact it is possible to tell an entire story simply through the dialogue, without anything else. Mostly, though, an author will tell part of the story through direct reporting of what happens and what the characters do, and part through what they say. Character is also revealed through what people say. You will probably want to use dialogue in both these ways.

MAKE IT REAL

Your dialogue, or speech, will need to be realistic. Ask yourself, would this person really say that? Have I heard people speak like that? Could I imagine myself saying it?

You will also need to consider who is speaking. Is what he or she is saying the kind of thing that we expect that particular character to say? Is it in keeping with the character? (For example, an old woman would speak very differently from a young boy. If your character is a bad-tempered person, the speech should sound bad-tempered; if he or she is a gentle, quiet person, the speech should fit that character – and so on.)

KEEP IT SHARP

Dialogue can be very dramatic – particularly in a scene with a quarrel, or where one speaker is threatening the other, or someone is terrified. On the other hand, don't put speech into your story just for the sake of it. The routine, trivial 'Goodbye, see you tomorrow,' 'Yeah, bye' kind of exchange is unnecessary. Leave it out.

PUNCTUATE IT ACCURATELY!

Dialogue should of course always be punctuated properly, with speech marks, commas etc. in the appropriate places. Check out the rules in The Structure Of Language, page 76.

FOR PRACTICE

1. Write a piece of dialogue between two people who are having an argument. Build it up from a moment of disagreement into a blazing row.

2. Write a dialogue where one person has all the power and status and is in command, and the other is nervously making excuses and trying to put him or herself back into the powerful person's good books.

3. Write a dialogue where one person is very upset and the other is trying to comfort him or her.

PLOT

In order for there to be a story at all, SOMETHING HAPPENS. The best kinds of plot for a short story are very simple ones. For example:

a. Boy finds treasure; boy nearly loses treasure; boy wins treasure in the end.

b. Lonely and crusty old man meets two children; they try to befriend him; he refuses them at first; gradually they win him round; something happens to them; he saves them.

c. Two friends; a third person appears on the scene; he makes friends with one; the other is jealous; in a fight, the new friend stands up for the jealous one; harmony is restored and all three become friends.

d. Children overhear two men talking suspiciously; they follow them and report to police; men turn out to be totally innocent – all a misunderstanding; children get invited to visit boat/castle/art studio/whatever belonging to one of the men; just what main character needs to become sailor/historian/art student/whatever.

So how do you find a plot?

CONFLICT OR DIFFICULTY

The main thing to remember is that a story is always organised around a **conflict** of some kind. It may be a quarrel, a loss, a threat of danger, a setback to the hero's hopes, an enemy, a misunderstanding – but there will be something that goes wrong. The essence of the story is – how is the situation going to go wrong, and how is it going to get put right?

So having decided on your character, and put him or her into a situation (within a setting), you need to think up a difficulty for him or her to face: an enemy, a danger, a disappointment – whatever it might be.

THE CLASSIC PLOT STRUCTURE

You will discover if you read a few that all stories have the same basic structure, falling into four distinct stages. They may vary in length and importance, but they will all be present.

INTRODUCTION

The first part of your story will introduce the characters and the situation. This is the **introduction**.

DEVELOPMENT

Then you will develop the story, building it up towards the conflict. This is called the **development**, or **complication**.

CLIMAX

Then you bring the story to its **climax** – the conflict is at its height. This is the dramatic high point of the story.

RESOLUTION

Finally, you tell how your hero gets out of his or her difficulties – how the conflict is resolved. This part of the story is called the **resolution**. If the story has a tragic resolution, it ends with the hero's defeat or even death. If there is a happy ending, the resolution restores harmony.

Every story has these four stages: introduction, development, climax and resolution.

Even a very simple story like *Jack and Jill* falls into these stages.

> Jack and Jill went up the hill – **introduction**
> To fetch a pail of water – **development**
> Jack fell down and broke his crown – **climax**
> And Jill came tumbling after – **resolution**

A most tragic tale! (You might like to analyse one or two other nursery stories in this way.)

So – you think of a situation of conflict for your character or characters to face. Work out how you are going to bring them to the climax. Then decide where you want to leave the situation at the end. You need to give careful thought to each of the four stages of the story.

But before you write the story itself, we need to think a little about –

THE END!

How people love writing those two words: THE END. Strangely enough, it is often the ending of a story which makes the difference between a really good story and a not-so-good one. Never rush your ending: this aspect needs at least as much, if not more, careful thought as all the rest.

THE TWIST OF SURPRISE

One of the best kinds of ending is the one with **a twist of surprise**. (For example, the story on page 21 has a lovely surprise ending.) Or you might want to end with a **question**, or a statement that leaves the reader with a question: 'Would I ever get home to my wife and children again, I wondered.' It can also be very effective to leave the ending **open**, so that the reader is not exactly sure whether the story ends happily or not: 'When I looked back, she was still standing there, waiting.'

NOT THE DREAM ENDING...

One very popular type of ending is the one which goes, 'So it had all been a dream' or 'And then I woke up'. This is a bit of a cop-out. It's just too easy, and it has been used too often. You should respect your reader enough to give your story a well thought out ending, not one which says, 'I've had enough of this and now I want to watch television, so I'm just going to opt out. Sorry.'

END WITH A FLOURISH

You may well find it best to leave the exact form of your ending until you get there. But once you do, you should always end with a satisfying flourish of some sort. Often a very short sentence is best. '"Well," he thought, "That's it." He turned and walked away.' or 'Slowly, she put the phone down.' or 'And that was the last I saw of him.'

So, now you're ready to WRITE YOUR STORY!
Good luck.

FOR PRACTICE

1. Analyse some of the books or stories you have read into the four stages. What is the main conflict? How does the story lead up to it? Where does the climax happen? What is the resolution? You may also like to read the story on page 21, asking yourself the same questions.

2. Plan two or three skeleton stories along the lines described, preferably each one in a different genre. Keep a notebook handy to jot down any good story plans that come to you. Nothing is more annoying than to have a brilliant idea for a story, and then find that because you didn't write it down at the time you can't remember it.

3. Write a full-length story in draft. Read it through aloud, so that you can hear it for yourself. Consider how it might be improved. Perhaps try out one or two different endings.

4. Write the final version.

If you produce enough good stories, you might consider putting them together to make a book – or even, if they are really good, sending them off to a publisher. Who knows, maybe you will be a famous author one day...

A LAST WORD

If you are the kind of person who gets an idea for a story and just 'sees' it whole before you have written a word, you can probably afford to ignore everything on this topic. You are probably doing it all naturally anyway. You might find it useful to read it all anyhow, and see if you agree with it. But you should never let well-meaning teachers' 'formulas' or 'recipes' or rules for writing get in the way of real inspiration. Some people are natural born writers. If you're one of them, just keep writing. The more you practise and nurture your talent, the better you'll be as a writer.

THE BICYCLE

It happened when I was six years old, in an old, rusty, disused garage that smelt strongly of mouldy shoe polish, when the sight met my eyes that was going to make the biggest change in my boring life.

I was not naturally bored; my mother told me every day that I would not be bored if I tried harder to be interested. Sometimes, when I flicked through the books that my desperate teacher gave me, in the hope of interesting me, the thought came to me that a change was going to occur soon, my boredom was extinguishable, an obstacle waiting to be overcome.

At the back of the garage was a bicycle. Bright words below the saddle read: THE EXPLORER. The bicycle was silver and had a lot of strange buttons on the handle. A sign was popped up against a rusty tin of paints that caught my eye:

THE EXPLORER
This bike is unique with a brake in the first place that you look in an emergency; eg: on the handlebars, under the saddle, on the pavement, up a tree etc...
There are many features including
  • Unfolding wings (two at the back, two at the front)
  • Missiles (these do not kill, they only have stink pellets in them)
  • A handle (for bumpy rides or dives)
  • Car horn and earphones (wear them - the noise can be up to 300 watts)
  • Air bags and a crash helmet
  • Blanket and pillows (for night journeys)
  • Fizzy drinks and hot cocoa (stored in containers on the frame)
  • Pocket calculator, diary, sketch book etc...
  • Parachute
  • Toothbrush and toothpaste.
NOTE: Do not use any of these special features unless you are sure what will happen when they function.

WARNING: This is not a toy, do not treat it like a joke.

'Wow!,' I thought, my long lost interest appearing with a pop.

Just as I was wondering what the price of the bike was, and counting the few bronze coins that were jangling in my pockets, a door opened in the back of the garage. The door creaked, as if it had not seen a can of oil for at least thirty years, and it wobbled uncontrollably (the whole garage looked as if it might collapse on my head). A old man walked shakily in.

He was a short man, who walked with a limp. He had a stick and a short, bristly white beard. He had a very bad case of Parkinson's disease. When he walked towards the bike, his stick wobbled onto a spot of polish that had spilt on the floor, his stick slid forwards and he very nearly fell over.

'So. You have your eye on this bicycle, boy?'
I jumped. I was feeling nervous and quivery. I felt an uneasiness about this old man. I spoke quietly and shakily. 'Yes,' I said.
'This very bicycle?' he asked.
'Yes,' I replied nervously.
'It will cost you every coin in your pockets ....and a little more,' he said with a greedy glint in his eye.
'I only have eleven pence and my train fare home,' I said glumly, in a very small voice.
'Do you need the train fare?' every muscle in the old man's body twitched, and his eyes were hungry-looking, like staring into the eyes of a starved wolf.
'Yes, but if I gave it to you, my mother could give me some more money for a ticket,' I said quickly. I wanted to go and find my mother, wanted to stay away from that man, but I had a burning desire; to have that bike. It seemed the only thing that was important was to have it.....and yet...

'Thomas!,' a voice shouted, 'Thomas, where are you? Its time to go now!'
'Mum!,' I shouted back, 'Wait a moment!'

But the old man had gone. Vanished. Disappeared into thin air.

I left one pound and eleven pence on the floor and wheeled my prize out of the door. The instruction manual hovered over the handle bars, wobbling when I lifted the bike over the wet polish on the floor that the old man had stumbled on.

My mother seemed in a frightful state. I had wandered aimlessly away when she had stopped to get some stamps at the post office. I had been going to look in the windows of an inviting looking sweet shop on the main road, but before I could get to the door, I turned around and stumbled upon the old garage. I had been in there for at least half an hour before she called me.

'Half an hour of frantic worry, who knows what could have happened to you, wandering around the community, you could have drowned in the Thames, got lost, died or ....,' my mother stopped while her brain thought of some more drastic ends.

My mother did not notice the bike, she was too upset. She did not even glance at it, gleaming in my hands. She just frog-marched me back to the station, took me home, and hurried upstairs to father muttering fiercely to herself words such as: 'So worried about you,' and 'never of thought of it of you.'

This was the moment I had been waiting for, to try out the bike...

Several weeks later, I had managed to ride the bike many times. Flying it was quite difficult because you had to keep your balance. I worked out this, after diving off the house roof, to my mother's great distress. I found out how to use all the basic things and I discovered that I could deep-sea dive rather well. The fishes in the garden pond were much disturbed but other than that, no one minded.

The parachute was very necessary, as I needed lots of practise before I could fly the bike well. It billowed out when the bike felt itself falling, or in danger. All the buttons were for different things, for example: The cocoa had a container which spurted the cocoa in my face if I was not alert, or the calculator leaked large plastic letters if I pressed two buttons at once.

All in all, this bike had been the only thing in the world that had interested me and I was not prepared to share it with anyone. I became sulky and bad tempered, and I was rude to my parents when they prevented me from riding it. It was no surprise that two months after the meeting in the garage, a letter came that stated quite plainly: Bring the bike back to the garage.

I did not write back or sulk because I couldn't ride to the garage this time.

After school one day, I took the bike back to the garage and placed it back against the peeling brick walls. Then I turned around with a last look at the bike, and walked out.

Suddenly a great view met my eyes. Everything seemed so new, so inviting, so ....interesting....'Mum! Come on! I want to go on the swings in the park! I want to say hello to the bus conductor! I want to...,' but my words were lost in the roar of the traffic.

But still, in the distance ....a young boy hugged his mother and stepped out on to the beginning of a fresh, beautiful new world. Behind the boy, a familiar old man winked and vanished into the atmosphere.

Emily Labram, aged 10

INTRODUCTION

When playwrights or script writers create their work, their aim, just as that of the novelist or short story writer, is to tell a story. So of course all the same elements apply: plot, characters, settings etc. Here, however, the story is told in a different way; there are no descriptions or explanations: we are shown the setting; we see the characters. But the story is told solely through **action** and **dialogue**.

> ### DON'T TELL ME, SHOW ME!
> This has important implications. The script writer or dramatist cannot explain to us what a person is thinking, or what his motives are. He has to show us. The novelist or short story writer can take us right inside her characters' heads – inside their souls. But in the theatre or on the screen we have to discover what the character is thinking by observing his actions, his body language, and above all what he says.

MAKING A SCENE

Plays written for the theatre are usually divided into whole scenes. A change of scene might mean a change to a different place, or a change in time – for example, the next morning. The action on stage during each whole scene is understood to be taking place in a particular setting – within a room, perhaps, or a garden, or the street – until the scene changes.

Modern dramatists have tried in many different ways to break free of the restrictions of the traditional stage set. Props and lighting can suggest where the scene is supposed to be, and the actors can often move freely from one 'scene' to another on the same stage, without any need for interrupting the action. However, that is mostly up to the director, not the writer. In writing a drama script, you would normally divide it into distinct scenes. At the start of each scene, you state the scene number, then the place and time of the action. For example: 'Scene 2. The street outside the prison. Morning.'

SETTING AND STAGE DIRECTIONS

Although you can't actually describe the scene for your audience, you can give directions as to how you want it. For example, you might start at the top of your first scene with something like this.

> *The living room in the Wilsons' London house. It is a bright spring morning, and sunlight is pouring in through a window at stage left. The room is untidy, with toys scattered about the floor. There is a tray full of last night's supper things still on the table. Jason is sitting sprawled in an easy chair with a newspaper spread out in front of him. Offstage, we can hear children playing noisily.*

Again, although you can't tell us what what your actors are thinking and feeling, you can give stage directions to the actors tell them what actions to perform and what sort of expression to use as they speak their lines. You might, for instance, write something like this:

The phone rings. Jason looks annoyed. He puts down his paper carefully, gets up and walks over to pick up the receiver.

Jason: Hullo. (He starts.) Oh my God, it's you! Where are you? Are you OK? What…? What……?! Oh. Hullo. Hullo!… (He listens for a moment, then puts the receiver down.) Damn. (He stands looking worried and uncertain for a minute or two. Then he shouts to someone offstage.) Jenny! I've got to go out.

Enter Julie. She is about 12 years old, and has long blond hair.

Julie: Dad? Where are you going?

Jason: Doesn't matter. Tell Mum I won't be in for lunch.

He rushes out and we hear the front door slam.

We don't know who was on the other end of the line, or what Jason is thinking. But we are immediately aware of a rise in **dramatic tension** as he realises who it is. Dramatic tension arises from a conflict of some kind. Just as with story-telling, **conflict** is a central element in the creation of drama. Already in this short extract, we have begun to pick up clues that something is going to go wrong, and we want to know what's going to happen.

ADAPTATION

One favourite of some teachers is to ask you to re-write a scene from a book you are reading in class as a piece of drama. You need to remember that you can only really use the **characters' actual speech** from the book. The skill is to write the stage directions in such a way that your play captures the original scene as closely as possible.

LAYOUT

On page 25 you will find an example of the correct layout for a drama script. It is important to follow this when you write in the form of drama.

FOR PRACTICE

1. Using the correct layout, write a scene from a play about a girl or boy going to a new school for the first time. Remember – dramatic tension!

2. Using the correct layout, write a scene involving two people who have been captured by a rebel army and are plotting their escape.

3. Take a chapter or section from one of your favourite books and turn it into a playscript. Remember – don't tell me, show me!

LAYOUT SHEET 1 – DRAMA SCRIPT

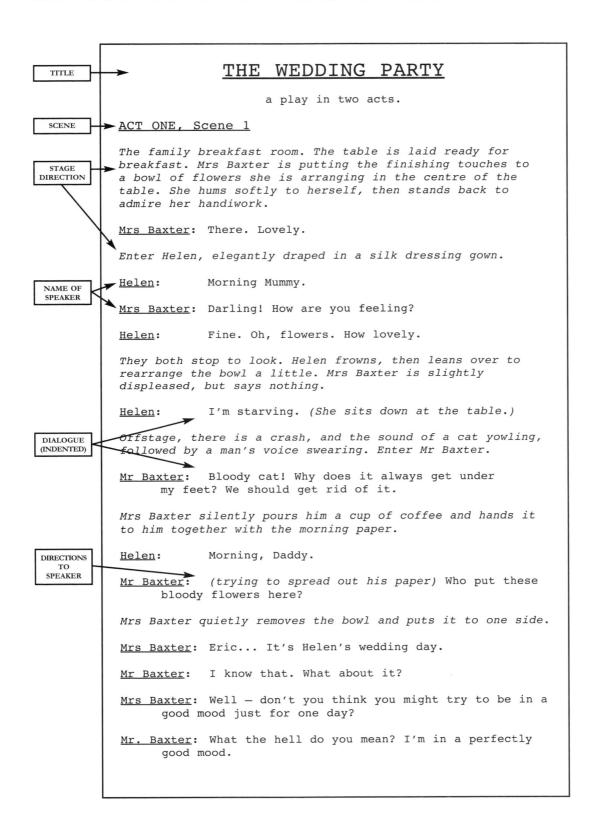

TITLE	**THE WEDDING PARTY**

a play in two acts.

SCENE → ACT ONE, Scene 1

STAGE DIRECTION → *The family breakfast room. The table is laid ready for breakfast. Mrs Baxter is putting the finishing touches to a bowl of flowers she is arranging in the centre of the table. She hums softly to herself, then stands back to admire her handiwork.*

Mrs Baxter: There. Lovely.

Enter Helen, elegantly draped in a silk dressing gown.

NAME OF SPEAKER → Helen: Morning Mummy.

Mrs Baxter: Darling! How are you feeling?

Helen: Fine. Oh, flowers. How lovely.

They both stop to look. Helen frowns, then leans over to rearrange the bowl a little. Mrs Baxter is slightly displeased, but says nothing.

Helen: I'm starving. *(She sits down at the table.)*

DIALOGUE (INDENTED) → *Offstage, there is a crash, and the sound of a cat yowling, followed by a man's voice swearing. Enter Mr Baxter.*

Mr Baxter: Bloody cat! Why does it always get under my feet? We should get rid of it.

Mrs Baxter silently pours him a cup of coffee and hands it to him together with the morning paper.

DIRECTIONS TO SPEAKER → Helen: Morning, Daddy.

Mr Baxter: *(trying to spread out his paper)* Who put these bloody flowers here?

Mrs Baxter quietly removes the bowl and puts it to one side.

Mrs Baxter: Eric... It's Helen's wedding day.

Mr Baxter: I know that. What about it?

Mrs Baxter: Well — don't you think you might try to be in a good mood just for one day?

Mr. Baxter: What the hell do you mean? I'm in a perfectly good mood.

INTRODUCTION

You probably won't be asked to do this very often, but it is fun to do, and worth knowing about. After all, you might just end up with a career in the movies...

WATCH THE SCREEN

Many of the same things apply as we discussed in relation to drama scripts. Again, you have to show rather than tell. The only thing the audience can know is **what it sees on screen**, or what a character reveals on screen during a dialogue.

But there is less need for dialogue in a film. You can tell a lot of a story just by having the camera follow it. Nobody says much during a car chase, for example. And many films begin with a street scene in which the audience only gradually becomes aware of which figure in the crowd is the one they need to watch.

CHANGING SCENES

In a movie you can have mountains, rivers, cities, oceans – or any brand of fantasy from outer space if you choose. But every time the camera moves to a new scene – say, from inside the front door of a flat to the landing outside, then from the landing to inside the lift – you have a new scene.

At the start of each scene you give the scene number. Then you specify 'INT' (for interior, or indoors) or 'EXT' (for exterior, or outside), then you give the place, followed by DAY or NIGHT. So the little sequence described above might look in a script like this:

```
43. INT. FRONT HALL IN JEFF's FLAT. DAY
JEFF goes to table, picks up keys, opens door, goes out.
                                              CUT TO:
44. INT. LANDING. DAY
JEFF crosses landing, presses lift button. Waits. Lift arives.
He gets into it.
                                              CUT TO:
45. INT. INSIDE LIFT. DAY
JEFF in lift. He consults his watch, looks anxious.
```

LAYOUT

The film industry is very particular about the layout of film scripts. So it's important to get it right. Have a look at the layout on page 27. It may also answer some of your questions about the series of scenes above. You may have wondered, for instance, why every time the character's name appears, it is written in capitals.

FOR PRACTICE
Go on. Enjoy yourself. Write a sequence of scenes from the film you would really love to make.

LAYOUT SHEET 2 – FILM SCRIPT

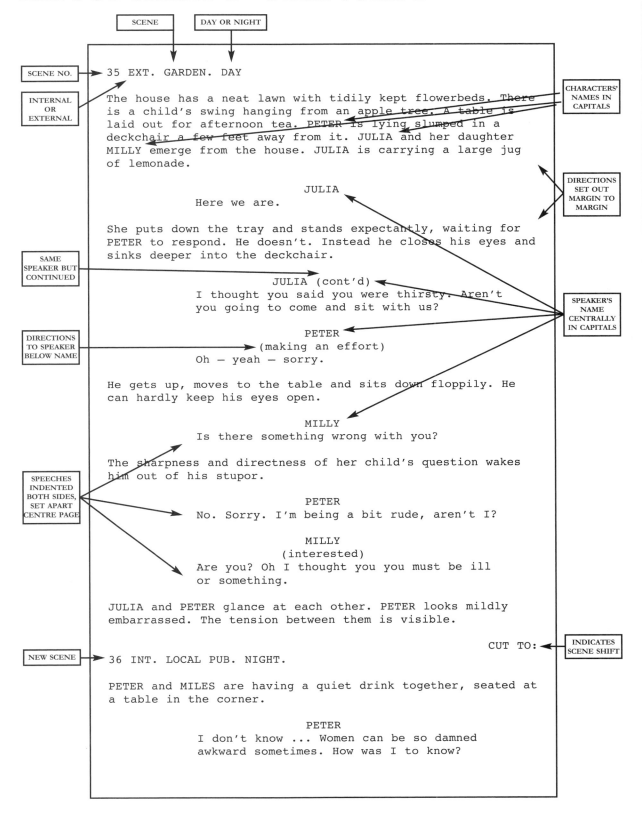

SCENE

DAY OR NIGHT

SCENE NO.

INTERNAL OR EXTERNAL

35 EXT. GARDEN. DAY

The house has a neat lawn with tidily kept flowerbeds. There is a child's swing hanging from an apple tree. A table is laid out for afternoon tea. PETER is lying slumped in a deckchair a few feet away from it. JULIA and her daughter MILLY emerge from the house. JULIA is carrying a large jug of lemonade.

CHARACTERS' NAMES IN CAPITALS

DIRECTIONS SET OUT MARGIN TO MARGIN

                    JULIA
          Here we are.

She puts down the tray and stands expectantly, waiting for PETER to respond. He doesn't. Instead he closes his eyes and sinks deeper into the deckchair.

SAME SPEAKER BUT CONTINUED

                    JULIA (cont'd)
          I thought you said you were thirsty. Aren't you going to come and sit with us?

SPEAKER'S NAME CENTRALLY IN CAPITALS

                    PETER
DIRECTIONS TO SPEAKER BELOW NAME
          (making an effort)
          Oh — yeah — sorry.

He gets up, moves to the table and sits down floppily. He can hardly keep his eyes open.

                    MILLY
          Is there something wrong with you?

The sharpness and directness of her child's question wakes him out of his stupor.

SPEECHES INDENTED BOTH SIDES, SET APART CENTRE PAGE

                    PETER
          No. Sorry. I'm being a bit rude, aren't I?

                    MILLY
          (interested)
          Are you? Oh I thought you you must be ill or something.

JULIA and PETER glance at each other. PETER looks mildly embarrassed. The tension between them is visible.

                                        CUT TO:

INDICATES SCENE SHIFT

NEW SCENE

36 INT. LOCAL PUB. NIGHT.

PETER and MILES are having a quiet drink together, seated at a table in the corner.

                    PETER
          I don't know ... Women can be so damned awkward sometimes. How was I to know?

27

INTRODUCTION

There are as many ways of writing poetry as there are people. So what follows here are just a few hints to help get you started. There is also a selection of poems by Key Stage 3 pupils using different approaches to writing poetry.

WHAT IS POETRY?

This is not an easy question. Many great writers have offered an answer to it, but so far no-one has really come up with a definition about which everybody can agree. You could simply say that poetry is what we recognise as poetry when we see it. Or that it is different from prose (the ordinary kind of writing) because it is set out in verse These statements may be true, but they are not altogether helpful. Perhaps a better way to start would be to ask why, rather than writing prose, would you choose to write poetry?

WHAT INSPIRES YOU?

Perhaps you have seen something which strikes you as beautiful, or strange, or funny, or amazing, or sad. Perhaps you have felt something very deeply. Perhaps something has made you think in a quite new way. In other words, something has **inspired** you. And you want to express what you have seen and felt and thought. So you write a poem.

POETRY REQUIRES INTENSE CONCENTRATION

Poetry allows you to put things in a much more intense and concentrated way than prose. Not a single word must be allowed to intrude if it has no business to be in your poem. There is nothing vague or sloppy; on the contrary, your thoughts have to be pared down to the barest essentials. To write a true poem, you must concentrate like you have never concentrated before. You must listen to the words forming in your mind and heart, watching them out onto the page as if nothing else in the world mattered or existed.

DOES IT HAVE TO RHYME?

Definitely not. In fact, until you are fairly experienced it may be best not to use rhyme at all, unless it just happens by itself. Otherwise you may distort your poem in your effort to make the rhyme work. What the poem expresses is much more important than whether it rhymes. It's fun to use rhyme when you want to write a funny or light-hearted poem. Look at the two poems, C and D, on page 32. Both use rhyme in a quite playful way.

WHAT ABOUT RHYTHM?

Poets like to experiment using different poetic forms, different line and verse lengths, different patterns of rhyming, and different sorts of rhythm. We all learn to enjoy rhythmic speech and song from a very young age, in the form of nursery rhymes. And in fact all speech naturally has rhythm, but we don't notice it unless the rhythm is regular, as it is in a nursery rhyme. (Try saying one and clapping the rhythm.)

IT'S YOUR CHOICE

People have been writing poetry in English for the past fifteen centuries or so. During that time there have been periods when poetry has nearly all had regular rhyme and metre (or rhythm). At other times, particularly in the twentieth century, most poets have written 'free verse', that has no particular rhythm or form. You start a new line where it feels right. So it's really up to you whether your poems should 'scan' (that is, have a regular metre) or not.

But if you are a person who really enjoys writing poetry, it is well worth experimenting a little with different patterns. Look at a good poetry anthology to see what other poets have done.

GETTING STARTED – POEMS FROM POEMS

One excellent 'way in' is to take an idea from a poem you have read. Poems A and B on page 31 were inspired by 'To Paint the Portrait of a Bird' by Jacques Prevert. In both of them the writers reflect about the act of creating.

WHAT DO YOU SEE?
Try this. Look at something quite ordinary. Stare at it for a long time. Let your imagination work. What do you see? Be patient. Keep looking. Give the object your whole attention. Keep still. Gradually your imagination will start to produce a succession of thoughts or pictures. Write them down immediately. Don't count anything out. Then use these impressions to help you form a poem. Read poems E and F. on page 32. They were produced in this way.

THINK ABOUT IT!

Once you get the hang of looking at the world like this, and begin really to see it, you will find everything interesting. You'll never be bored again! The poems on pages 32 and 33 all came about because the writer looked at something quite ordinary, really saw it, and thought carefully about it. In poem G, it's an old pair of boots. The poet has looked at them and imagined how they might feel. (This is called 'personification' – a device that poem M on page 34 also uses.) In poem H, the poet considers the River Thames, and comes up with some fresh ideas. In poem I, the poet puts herself imaginatively 'inside' a slug! Poem J just catches that uneasy moment of fear – something we have all experienced – when you feel a little threatened and you're not quite sure what's going on.

What is special about these poems is not the object or event itself, but the way each poet has thought about it.

WHAT IS IT LIKE?

Another method for finding a poem is to concentrate on using a literary device. For instance, take a familiar object or situation and ask, what is it like? It's like a lot of things. Write them all down, till you have a whole list of similes. Then make a poem from your list. Poems K and L do just this.

GO ON – EXPERIMENT!

Poem N uses several devices. It personifies Death, uses similes and metaphors to describe 'him', as well as employing paradox – 'an unthought thought' 'a madman's sanity' – and alliteration 'like a lantern to lead you'. Poem N arose simply from an exercise in having fun with alliteration. Why don't you have a go at some of this?

LOOKING AT THE WIDER WORLD

The final three poems were all inspired by war – different conflicts in each case. Here, the poets have all imagined something which is actually beyond their immediate experience, but has touched them very deeply. Next time you hear something or see something in the news that goes to your heart, write a poem about it.

There are really no rules – so feel free!

POEMS FROM POEMS

A. THE BOOK

Pick up the book
Hold it how you want
With complete silence around you.
Begin to search the book with your eyes,
And be on friendly terms with it.
Let the words form a picture,
The picture a story
Which unravels and unwinds
The deeper you delve.
Yet the words might not form
The picture you expect;
It might take forms
Unexpected
And
Challenging.
Pictures of love, death and hate
All come together and are trapped
Inside the book.
The only way these emotions are revealed
Is if
Someone reads the book
So the picture can escape
And go directly to the thoughtplace.
From there the picture will plant a seed,
And this seed will develop,
Till the tentacles
Reach out
And touch other things
With the story.

Manisha Assanand, aged 13

B. I PAINT THE LADY

I find a canvas to paint upon,
I find a brush to spread my colour,
I find some pure water for my brush.

I look to find my inspiration.
An old lady with fine lines around her eyes,
Her hair grey,
With brush streaks of black colour through it.

I paint the lady with my brush,
Stroke by stroke up and down.
I build her up from a skeleton to have flesh,
To be a person
With a heart and feeling.

I paint my lady into a background
Of spring with flowers and sun.
She sits in a wooden rocking chair,
Where she watches the world float by,
Watching me the artist,
Watching you the people,
Watching our world at present.

Anoushka Tiagi, aged 13

RHYMING POEMS

C. THE MARK

Do I dare to see my mark?
I know it's dangerous,
Like a shark.
The thoughts of it being bad
Go round in my min,
They make me mad.

What if it's a D
Or E
Or maybe F?!

I dare not look,
Just in case.

Then again maybe I should
You never know
It might be good.
I open the page,
Shut my eyes…
Oh, it's such an age!

Then there it is,
A straight A.
Wow!
Well that's okay.
                    Lauren Crawley, Aged 11

D. PEOPLE

I like people
                    Because
Sometimes they are
                    Funny,
Sometimes they are
                    Sad;
Sometimes they are
                    Skinny,
Sometimes they are
                    Mad;
Sometimes they are
                    Fat,
Sometimes they are
                    Small.
But anyway, I like them
                    All.
                    Thomas Whiffen, aged 11

LOOKING POEMS

E. A COIN

It's a glass eye which doesn't see
The sun, a ball of brightness, the moon against
                                        a dark sky,
A planet with dust men on it.
Some earplugs when you hate the noise.
A means of decision, heads or tails.

When it spins it's a football;
When flat, the waste from a hole punch.
A tadpole's lily pad,
A gift of value,
Caesar's fat globe,
The monocle of a Victorian man,
A discus for an athlete.

A coin is a flying saucer for a mouse or an elf;
It's a frisbee to little people;
It's the wheel of a wheelchair for a rat.

Spinning or not, this is what I see.
                    Ben Harwood, aged 12

F. THE BANANA

As I look at the banana…

I see brown boulders visible on the yellow desert.
I see an arch-shaped boat sailing along the long
                                        roads of Venice.
I see a ramp where skateboarders can show off
                                        and impress.
I can see a crescent-shaped moon where the
                                        man who lives on it
Can easily sit and observe.
I see a purple bruise.
I see children playing on a see-saw.
I see an arch-shaped bridge.
I can see happiness in a certain perspective
And sadness in the opposite.

Now I feel hungry….
                    Anish Shah, aged 12

THINKING POEMS

G. OLD BOOTS

There they sit, that odoured pair,
Lazy and dirty, their arms draped
Around them, collapsed on the floor.
Old and useless, boots which were once
Up and running, fit and flash,
Now weak and dreary.
There they sit nattering,
Their red suede skin wrinkled and wintered,
Skin which was once soft and silky smooth.
Now rough and tattered,
Their rubber soles worn out.
Reena Patel, aged 10

H. THE RIVER

The river is dark and mysterious,
Even dangerous at times,
But not for fish -
Oh no, under and over the fish swing,
Never doubting for a moment
The strength of the tide.
The river has seen history in all its glory,
All the great kings and queens of old.
The river flows faster and faster
Until it reaches the sea.
Then it gushes out,
Out into the open sea.
The river travels over a wide spread of sea
Until
After millions of miles of travelling,
It comes back
For our own eyes to see,
In all its glory.
John Hockley, aged 11

I. SLUGS

We like the wet.
Our slimy bodies
Enjoy the misery.

Without damp soaking
Through our shrivelled skins,
We are nothing.

We are pests.
We eat anything green
That comes our way.

We pride ourselves
That our slimy bodies
Slither over stone,

Leaving a silky trail,
Beautiful, shimmering,
Betraying our path.

We're liked only by hedgehogs.
in the winter we flourish;
In the summer we die.
Alice Aldous, aged 13

J. EMPTY FEARS

What's that?

Footsteps echo,
Coming after me down the street,
An owner who pauses, who watches, who goes.
Who mocks at rational thought.
Waiting in the part where the
Light from the lamps
Doesn't quite meet.
Daisy Smith, aged 14

SIMILE POEMS

K. MY BROTHER

My brother is like a roaring MG car,
A never-ending loud drumbeat,
The heatwave of the summer.
My brother is like a kangaroo hopping around,
He will never stop until life ends.
He is like a pestering bee,
He is like a dream of a wild apple tree.
Michael Makonnen, aged 11

L. A CLASSROOM

A classroom is like a beehive, where there is no
limit to noise.
Like a colony of ants, ever working for their
endless duty.
Like a field of corn, swaying in the wind.
Like a humming bird, taking in nectar of learning.
Like a dictionary, with everlasting things to
remember.
Like a locomotive speeding towards the future.
Like the rapids of a river.
Like a door through to manhood.
Jason Lester, aged 12

PERSONIFICATION POEM

M. DEATH

He is the guide, like a lantern to lead you
through the mist.
He is the emblem of bad and good,
Like laughter that has swelled and calmed.
He is a madman's sanity and a sane man's
madness.
He is like a dying man, an unborn child.
He is an unthought thought or a plan in the
making.
He is a lark taking off or a sparrow nesting
Even the jay in flight.
He is like an unbroken promise, a sacred oath.
An end and a beginning.
He is the judge, jury and the cell.
An evening drawing in

Or a dawn breaking.
Michael Williams, aged 12

ALLITERATION POEM

N. SEA NYMPH

The river winds its wandering way
Like a ribbon of silver to the lonely little bay
From the high hill and the hidden vale
Through the ferny forest in the moonlight pale,
Now cascading into chasms, now sliding slow
Foaming and bubbling to the ocean far below.

And the nymph that follows is dancing free,
As she flees to her home in the shining sea.
Her white feet fly across the soft silver sand,
As the white waves crash on the waiting land.
And the sea-nymphs sing beneath the ocean's
roar,
As she bids the earth farewell, to return no more.
Anna Hopkins, aged 13

POEMS INSPIRED BY WAR

O. KOSOVO

An empty village all alone,
Once filled with voices and life.
Only the cry of a lost child lingers
Or the moan of a hungry dog
And the pain of the old who can't walk.

But the hope and the courage
That keeps them going,
And the love that makes them strong,
Is the secret of their survival
On a painful journey, which lasts so long.
Grace Aza Selinger, aged 13

P. THE DARKEST SHADOW

Where are they going?
Trains are cramped.
People stamped.
There's a whisper in the air.

People are anxious.
The wind is blowing.
The country's going.
The shadow's moving forwards.

In chaos and commotion,
The Panzer divisions arrive.
The smell of death and on they drive.
What for us: will we survive?
Thomas Glover, aged 10

Q. HOME BY CHRISTMAS

Go, I tell him, go,
Go and wear khaki,
Go, I tell him, go
Go fight for the glory of your country.

Chattering men in olive green suits
Stamp cards and give directions,
Directions to a weepy sea
Of gentle mothers holding red handkerchiefs.

'Join the army today' it says
In front of a crowd of boys,
Hopeful kids not knowing their fate
Pencilled on their souls.

Cavalry clattering into the train
Trampling mud, splashing babes,
Doors closing with a slam,
Ringing, rumbling, rattling.

They'll be back for Christmas,
Were the thoughts as the train departed.
They'll be back in the rackety ridden rain.
They'll be back for Christmas they will,
They will, they will – won't they?
Hannah Mowat, aged 13

INTRODUCTION

In this section you will learn how to use writing to convey information and to explain or describe facts and processes. This includes writing reports or factual articles, producing information leaflets and writing formal letters. For this kind of writing, obviously, you need information, and you need to be sure that it is accurate.

SOURCES OF INFORMATION

There are many different ways of finding out information, and you should be ready to use all or any of them. Here are some, but there may well be others.

• REFERENCE BOOKS

(For help on how to use reference books, see the Section on Study Skills, pages 68-71)

DICTIONARY
As well as the ordinary dictionary you use in class, there are **specialist dictionaries** on many subjects – dictionaries of art and artists, dictionaries of history, mythology, science etc. Your local library should have these.

ENCYCLOPAEDIA
Your school should have one. If not, try the local library.

HANDBOOK
There are many 'pocket book' versions of handbooks on all kinds of subjects available from most book shops.

COMPANION OR GUIDE
Look out for large reference books called 'The Companion to…' or 'The Guide to…' your subject.

• THE MEDIA

NEWSPAPERS
Look out for articles and pictures relevant to your topic, cut them out and keep them.

TELEVISION AND RADIO
Watch or listen to relevant programmes, and make notes. Remember especially to note the names of people you may want to quote.

FILMS
Occasionally you may find that a film contains material you can use.

• THE INTERNET

Search for a website on your topic. You may find there are hundreds, and your real difficulty is knowing how to select which ones to use! What you should **not** do, ever, is just copy an article from the internet. **ALWAYS** acknowledge your source. (See below.)

• OTHER PEOPLE

This is the most obvious source of information. If you know someone who has experience or information on your topic, ask them about it. (Remember always to quote them accurately if you want to use their actual words.) An eye-witness account, or first hand experience from an expert, will always make informative writing much more convincing.

USING INFORMATION

It is **absolutely vital** that whenever you use information you have obtained from any of these sources, you **acknowledge your source**. This means that if you quote the actual words from a book or any other written material, or what someone has said to you, you put them **within quotation marks** and state who wrote or spoke them.

ACCURATE QUOTATION

In the case of written material, you can put the author's name and the title of the book or paper in brackets after the quoted part. (Or, if you prefer, you can do this as a footnote – see page 57) If you are quoting someone's words 'live', you should say something like "When I spoke to John Smith, head of the museum's dinosaur section, he said, …'" Make quite sure you have quoted the **exact words**. If necessary, check with the person concerned, and get his or her permission to quote what they have said.

LAYOUT

This is most important, especially if you are creating something like an information leaflet. You want your readers to be able to absorb the information you are giving them as easily as possible, and to draw their attention to the more essential parts of it.

SPACE

Leave lots of free space on the page. Use generous margins, and leave spaces between paragraphs and between the heading and what follows it.

HEADING

This should generally be brief but striking and memorable. Put it in large, bold letters.

SUB-HEADINGS

These are useful to help guide your reader through the material. (You will see that this book, for instance, is full of them.)

BULLET POINTS

These help to

- focus the reader's attention,
- highlight important information

NUMBERING

It may be useful to use both letters and numbers when you want to divide a subject up into lots of sub-topics. There is quite a variety to choose from, using capitals (A,B), lower case (a,b), ordinary numbers (2, 15) Roman numerals (II, XV, or ii, xv), and italics (x, y). When you have decided on a numbering system, stick to it. For example:

Section A. Part 1: a) .. b)..; Part 2: a(i) ...a(ii)... (b)...

INDENTATION

If you are using lots of sections and sub-sections, it may be useful to **indent** them in a logical way. (Indent means place away from the margin, as you do for a new paragraph.) So

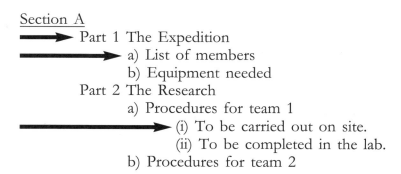

Section A
⟶ Part 1 The Expedition
⟶ a) List of members
b) Equipment needed
Part 2 The Research
a) Procedures for team 1
⟶ (i) To be carried out on site.
(ii) To be completed in the lab.
b) Procedures for team 2

ILLUSTRATIONS

By all means use photographs, drawings, diagrams etc. Try to design your page so that everything 'lines up' neatly. Don't leave bits sticking out awkwardly, out of line with the text.

BE BOLD!
There are many ways of drawing attention to particular words or sections. You can use CAPITAL LETTERS, or **bold type**, or *italics*, or underlining. Or you can put words in a box. Or, of course, you can use colour. Have fun. Make your information leaflet as striking and interesting to look at as you can.

SHAPE AND SIZE

You may want to use a larger sized paper – for a poster, for instance. Or, for a leaflet, you might want to fold your A4 sheet in half, or into three equal sections, so that you can design a front section and then the 'inside' parts.

FOR PRACTICE

1. Collect information for a leaflet on one of the following:

   a. Your favourite sport.
   b. A holiday place or adventure.
   c. Any subject that really interests you.

2. Write the text for your leaflet. Do this in rough.

3. Design your leaflet, using some of the methods suggested above.

4. Create the finished leaflet.

INTRODUCTION

The last section dealt with how to collect and use accurate information, and how to design an attractive layout. All of that is important when it comes to writing reports or articles too. But here are one or two further points to consider.

GUIDE YOUR READER

A useful way to start is with a paragraph stating the topics or areas your report is going to cover. Then work through each topic, giving a paragraph to each. (Use sub-headings, or any of the other techniques suggested on pages 38 and 39, if appropriate.)

BE CLEAR

Present your facts to start with clearly and with as few words as possible. Back up any statements you make with evidence in the form of facts and figures, showing where you got them from.

ROLL OUT THE EXPERTS

If you can, quote expert opinion to back up your own.

BE THOROUGH

In the case of a report, make sure you have properly and faithfully covered every aspect of the subject.

ENTERTAIN YOUR READER

In the case of an article, make it more lively and interesting with real-life stories, jokes if appropriate, and apt quotations.

FOR PRACTICE

1. Write a **report** on a school activity, such as sport, drama, debating etc., over the past year.

2. Write a **factual** article about one of the following (or a similar topic):

   a. Changes to your neighbourhood over the past 100 years.
   b. Your family's history.
   c. Children's crazes.

WRITING AN ESSAY

INTRODUCTION

What is an essay, and how do you set about writing one? The word 'essay' comes from the French word essayer, which means to try out or test something. So what you are really doing when you write an essay is trying out or testing your ideas about something. Writing your essay will give you a chance to consider the topic seriously, decide what you really think about it, and then put those thoughts into words on paper.

So – how do you start?

INFORMATIVE ESSAY

First of all, is it a topic which requires some **factual knowledge**? For instance, you might be asked to write about the history of your local area – or the person who invented, say, computers – or the attractions of tourism in a particular country – or education as it was in your grandparents' day. The possible list is of course endless, and if you have been given a topic of this kind, you will have to begin by doing a little **research**. Check out the hints on pages 72 on the best way of **doing research** and taking notes.

DISCURSIVE ESSAY

Or you may be asked to write an essay in which you **discuss** some current issue, or perhaps **persuade** your reader to agree with the point of view you are going to put forward.

This might be something like, 'Should boys and girls be educated separately?' or 'Does this country give refugees and asylum seekers a fair deal?' or 'Should parents have the right to smack their children?' Once again, you will need to get some facts together. It's no good discussing a topic, still less trying to persuade others to adopt your point of view, if you don't know what you are talking about. So first, make sure of your facts, and then, when you have looked at all the available evidence, decide what you think about the issue.

DESCRIPTIVE ESSAY

You are also likely to be asked to write a **descriptive** essay. This could be about, say, a winter landscape, or a crowded street market, or some place you know very well. This is in some ways easier, because you already have all the information you need. All you have to do is 'go there' in your mind, and describe what you see. All the same, you need to spend a little time preparing, thinking about the different aspects you might want to bring out, and what is the most effective way to present them.

REFLECTIVE ESSAY

Finally, there is the **reflective** essay – the one that asks you to reflect upon a topic like 'Solitude' or 'Coming Home' or 'Growing Up', and set down your thoughts about it. This too will need careful thought and preparation.

So – you have your topic. What next?

ASKING QUESTIONS

Now you need to make a pile of material, some of which you will use, but some you may decide to leave out. If you essay is on a factual topic, then the beginning part is easy – you create your 'pile' from your researches. But if you don't know where to begin, one useful way to start is by asking yourself questions.

What? Who? When? Where? How? Why?

What is X (your topic)? Who (what kind of people, or what particular person or persons) is involved in X? When does X happen, or when did it happen? Where is X to be found? How does X work, or how is it made, or how do people interact with it? And, probably the most important question, why X?

THINK ABOUT YOUR SUBJECT

In the case of a descriptive essay, for example, you might want to think about what your chosen scene is. (E.g. 'Andros is an island just off the coast of Greece.') Or *what kind* of things might you see there? Or *what kind* of experiences might you have there? *Who* lives there? Or *who* do you know there? *What sort* of life do people have there? *When* do you visit it? Or *when* was it discovered? Or *when* did it begin to change? *Where* is it? *How* do you get there? or *How* do people there live? *Why* have you chosen to write about it? Or *why* do you love it – or hate it?

COLLECTING THE INFORMATION

You get the idea? By the time you have gone through this process, you will at least have quite a bit to write about. You may want to collect all this in the form of a 'spider graph' or 'mind map', or just write it down as a list in whatever order it comes to you. When you are satisfied that you have a sufficient 'pile', you need to decide what parts of it you want to use.

So –

A PARAGRAPH (OR TWO) PER TOPIC

Each topic (and you may have many more than 5, but should try to have at least 4) will have a paragraph to itself. It may take up 2 or 3, depending on how much you have to say. So the plan above would generate at least seven paragraphs.

DECIDE WHAT TO INCLUDE

Now, from your original 'pile' (and anything further that may have occurred to you since), decide roughly what is going to go into each topic or paragraph. Jot this down on your plan, so that you remember.

WHERE'S YOUR EVIDENCE?

If your essay is on a subject for **discussion** or aims to present an **argument**, you will need to take particular care that each topic is backed up with evidence, facts, 'quotes' from authoritative sources, examples, etc. You can incorporate all these into your plan. Use very brief notes, just enough to remind yourself. (For example: 'Times quote.' 'Hosp. info.') **Don't make the mistake** of writing your whole essay in your plan.

When you have completed this whole process to your own satisfaction, you are **READY TO BEGIN**.

START HERE

Take a clean sheet of paper, write your name, the date and the title of your essay at the top.

WAIT FOR IT

Now – put down your pen, sit back, and let your mind go quiet. Slowly, without any hurry, bring it to focus on your essay topic. What is going to be your first sentence? This is all important. Wait for it – don't rush.

LISTEN

In a moment or two you will hear a sentence forming in your mind. Write it down, if you like, on a spare piece of paper – the bottom of your plan will do. Listen to it again. Is it exactly right? Does it sound interesting, lively, challenging? Is it going to make your reader want to read on? Only when you are quite satisfied that your opening sentence is **just right**, write it down.

Continue to listen as you write the next sentence, and the next, until your Introduction is complete. Read it over. Have you said all that you intended to say? Change it or add to it if you need to.

BACK TO THE PLAN

Now go back to your plan. Topic 1. How are you going to introduce it? Listen again, then write. Bring in all the facts, evidence etc. you noted in your plan. Or, if you are writing a descriptive or reflective essay, concentrate totally on 'seeing' what you are writing about. When your paragraph is finished, read it over, change it if necessary, add anything you may have left out. Consult your plan again and go on to the next topic.

LINKING YOUR PARAGRAPHS

Continue like this, linking each paragraph or topic with the one before by means of 'linking phrases'. For example,

'Another time, I…'
'This may be true, but…'
'On the other hand…'
'However…'
'Another interesting question is…'

YOUR CONCLUSION

When you have reached the end of your planned topics, stop again. How are you going to finish off your essay? It may require a full conclusion – especially if you have set out to discuss an issue or persuade your reader of a certain point of view. You may want to bring the point home, giving it a final, triumphant emphasis. Or you may only need to give your essay a final flourish to bring it to a satisfying end. This could be just a single sentence, like 'one thing is certain: silence is becoming more and more rare.' Or 'how many of today's busy commuters, I wonder, ever stop to think about the people who once lived here and made it what it has become?'

A LASTING IMPRESSION

You should take as much care with your final sentence as you did with your opening one, because this will be the lasting impression that your readers take away with them.

FOR PRACTICE

1. Choose 3 or 4 topics from this list and spend five minutes making a 'pile' or drawing a 'spider graph' or 'mind map' for each one:

> A room of my own; Growing up; Who are the heroes today?; A person I admire; What makes an ideal parent; Being homeless; Courage; Bullying; What kind of world do we want?; How I would change my school/city/country; Friends; What makes me angry.

2. Take a subject, divide it into a number of aspects or topics and make an outline plan. Make notes of what to include under each topic.

3. On a subject which interests you – perhaps something currently being talked about in the news – write a full-blown essay, following the steps described above.

A LAST WORD
Finally, read through your whole essay again, checking for mistakes. Try to ensure that your punctuation and spelling are 100% accurate, and that all your sentences are grammatically sound and complete. Make any minor alterations you may feel are necessary. Then... HAND IT IN!

INTRODUCTION

People have been sending letters to each other ever since writing was invented. But depending on the kind of message and the person to whom you are writing, the rules for writing letters vary.

PERSONAL LETTERS

These might range from a letter to thank your Aunt Clara for the birthday present she sent you, to an almost book-length account of the adventures you had on your round the world trip. Some letter-writers, especially before telephones and computers, wrote such brilliant and fascinating letters that they were later collected together and published. And some of the first novels were written in the form of a series of letters.

ADDRESS AND SALUTATION

The rules for personal letters are very few, and it doesn't really matter whether you follow them or not. But the normal way to set them out is to put your **address** and the **date** (even if it's 'Half way up Mount Everest, Sunday') at the top, on the right hand side of the paper. Then you write the **salutation** – that is, 'Dear Fred,' or whatever it is – on the next line on the left, and put a comma after it. Then you're off.

SIGN OFF

Most personal letters will end with the word 'Love from', or just 'Luv', but you can put whatever you like of course. Whatever it is, it will normally be on a line by itself, to the left or in the middle. And below it, you **sign** your name.

FORMAL LETTERS

The rules for these are a little more complicated. It is important to follow them if you want to give a good impression.

FAITHFULLY OR SINCERELY?

The most important thing to remember is that if you begin the letter with 'Dear Sir' or 'Dear Madam' (in other words you don't know the person by name), you should end it with the words 'Yours faithfully", but if you begin with 'Dear Mr Smith' (or Mrs, Miss, Ms, Dr. or whatever the person's correct title may be), you should end with 'Yours sincerely'.

FIND THE RIGHT TONE

For a formal letter, you need to use an appropriately formal style and tone. You should be courteous and respectful – even if you are writing to complain!

> **BE PRECISE**
> Avoid chatty, slangy or familiar language. It's also best to resist the temptation to try to be funny. Any such attempt is likely to fall very flat at the receiving end! Be clear and to the point.

YOU CAN'T BE TOO POLITE

If you are writing a polite, semi-formal letter addressed to someone you don't know well enough to call by their first name, you should still put your address and the date at the top, but there's no need to put in the address of the person to whom you are writing. Just start, 'Dear Mr Jones' – or whatever is the person's correct title. You should sign yourself off at the bottom with 'Yours sincerely' or 'Best wishes'.

These rules may seem old-fashioned and unnecessary to you, but there is no harm in keeping to them. Better to be thought well-mannered than rude and ignorant!

> **FOR PRACTICE**
> **1.** Write a letter to a firm of printers asking if they would be interested in producing your school's magazine, and requesting them to quote a price for the job.
>
> **2.** Write a letter to Mr Hogben, the owner of your local bookshop, apologising for recent ill-mannered behaviour in his shop by some pupils (including yourself!) from your school.

SET IT OUT CORRECTLY

On pages 48 and 49 you will see examples of the correct layout for formal business letters – one for when you don't know the name of the person your are addressing, and one for when you do.

LAYOUT – FORMAL LETTERS 1

1. Formal or business letters, where you do not know the name of the person you are addressing.

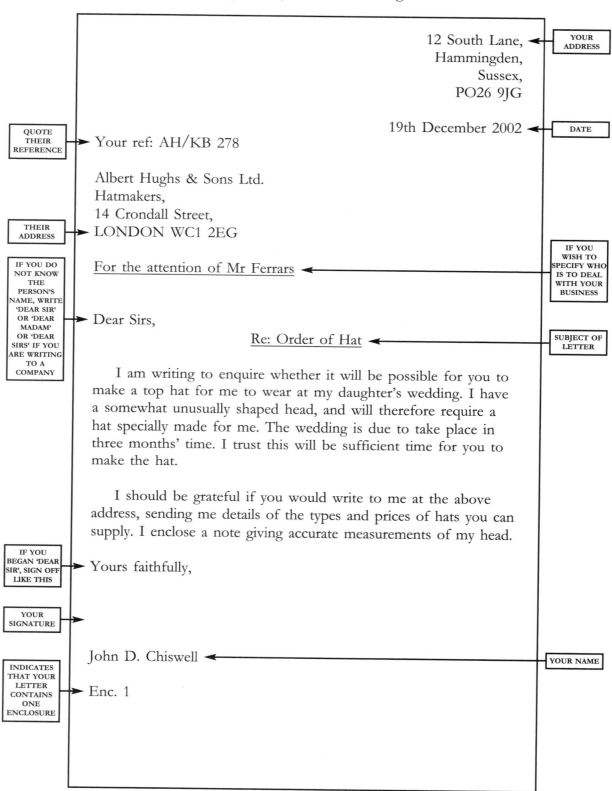

YOUR ADDRESS

12 South Lane,
Hammingden,
Sussex,
PO26 9JG

DATE

19th December 2002

QUOTE THEIR REFERENCE

Your ref: AH/KB 278

THEIR ADDRESS

Albert Hughs & Sons Ltd.
Hatmakers,
14 Crondall Street,
LONDON WC1 2EG

IF YOU WISH TO SPECIFY WHO IS TO DEAL WITH YOUR BUSINESS

For the attention of Mr Ferrars

IF YOU DO NOT KNOW THE PERSON'S NAME, WRITE 'DEAR SIR' OR 'DEAR MADAM' OR 'DEAR SIRS' IF YOU ARE WRITING TO A COMPANY

Dear Sirs,

SUBJECT OF LETTER

Re: Order of Hat

I am writing to enquire whether it will be possible for you to make a top hat for me to wear at my daughter's wedding. I have a somewhat unusually shaped head, and will therefore require a hat specially made for me. The wedding is due to take place in three months' time. I trust this will be sufficient time for you to make the hat.

I should be grateful if you would write to me at the above address, sending me details of the types and prices of hats you can supply. I enclose a note giving accurate measurements of my head.

IF YOU BEGAN 'DEAR SIR', SIGN OFF LIKE THIS

Yours faithfully,

YOUR SIGNATURE

YOUR NAME

John D. Chiswell

INDICATES THAT YOUR LETTER CONTAINS ONE ENCLOSURE

Enc. 1

LAYOUT – FORMAL LETTERS 2

2. Formal or business letters, where you know the name of the person you are addressing.

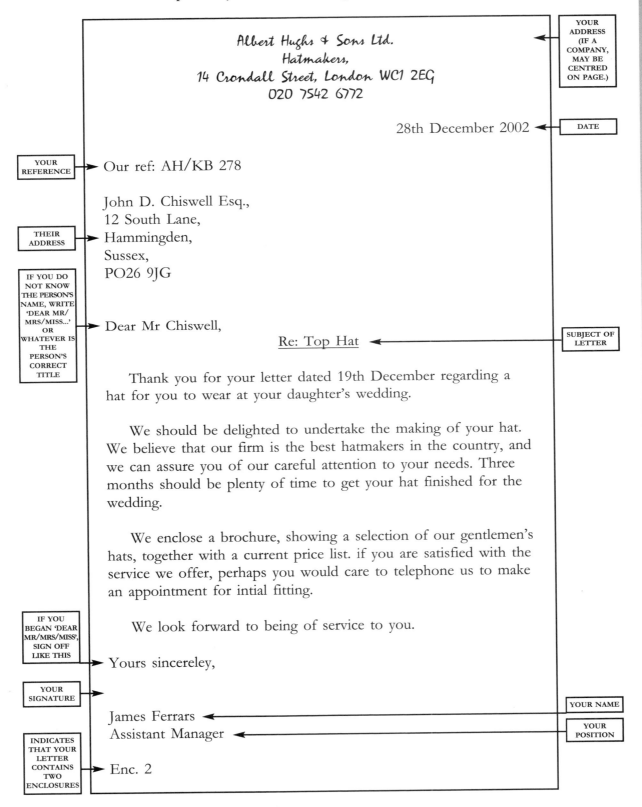

YOUR ADDRESS (IF A COMPANY, MAY BE CENTRED ON PAGE.)

Albert Hughs & Sons Ltd.
Hatmakers,
14 Crondall Street, London WC1 2EG
020 7542 6772

28th December 2002 — DATE

YOUR REFERENCE → Our ref: AH/KB 278

John D. Chiswell Esq.,
12 South Lane,
Hammingden,
Sussex,
PO26 9JG

THEIR ADDRESS

IF YOU DO NOT KNOW THE PERSON'S NAME, WRITE 'DEAR MR/MRS/MISS...' OR WHATEVER IS THE PERSON'S CORRECT TITLE

Dear Mr Chiswell,

Re: Top Hat ← SUBJECT OF LETTER

Thank you for your letter dated 19th December regarding a hat for you to wear at your daughter's wedding.

We should be delighted to undertake the making of your hat. We believe that our firm is the best hatmakers in the country, and we can assure you of our careful attention to your needs. Three months should be plenty of time to get your hat finished for the wedding.

We enclose a brochure, showing a selection of our gentlemen's hats, together with a current price list. if you are satisfied with the service we offer, perhaps you would care to telephone us to make an appointment for intial fitting.

We look forward to being of service to you.

IF YOU BEGAN 'DEAR MR/MRS/MISS', SIGN OFF LIKE THIS

Yours sincereley,

YOUR SIGNATURE

James Ferrars ← YOUR NAME
Assistant Manager ← YOUR POSITION

INDICATES THAT YOUR LETTER CONTAINS TWO ENCLOSURES

Enc. 2

INTRODUCTION

In this section you learn how to construct a coherent **argument**, or **persuade** your reader to agree with a point of view, or feel something.

CONSTRUCTING AN ARGUMENT

To argue your case effectively, you need to present a series of well ordered **reasons**, backed up by **evidence**.

• BEGIN EACH PARAGRAPH WITH A LINKING PHRASE.

It is important to **structure** your argument in a logical way so that a reader can follow it step by step. Lead your readers firmly through the argument, giving them 'signposts' in the form of linking phrases at the beginning of each paragraph.

Let us consider... Secondly... On the other hand... I should like to suggest...

Some linking words and phrases you may find useful:

Firstly... Next... Finally... If....then. Surely... Of course... Although...nonetheless... Since....., it follows that...Yet....However, ...To put it another way...It may be argued that....but....Not only...but also... On the one hand...on the other hand...For example... For instance... Obviously... Alternatively... Similarly... What is more... There is no doubt that...

• STATE THE PROBLEM OR DILEMMA

Start with a punchy opening sentence. Elaborate on this as necessary, so that your reader can clearly understand the issues. This may take several paragraphs.

The problem is this... Firstly... Secondly... On the one hand... On the other hand... In addition...

• REINFORCE YOUR POINT

Having demonstrated that something new is needed, you may want to reinforce the idea before suggesting solutions.

This situation cannot, obviously, be allowed to continue. We need to change the system. The question is, how?

• DEAL WITH ANY RIVAL SOLUTIONS

There may be several possible solutions.

Some people have suggested... Others would argue...

If you want your reader to reject these, explain why.

The disadvantage with this is...

• PUT FORWARD YOUR OWN PROPOSITION

I should like to suggest... I put it to you that...

Explain your points carefully, step by step. This may take several paragraphs.

This approach has a number of advantages. First of all... Secondly... Not only... but also... Because... Therefore...

• GIVE ILLUSTRATIONS OR EXAMPLES TO SUPPORT YOUR POINTS.

Make these as vivid and effective as possible. You may want to cite facts, figures, 'expert' opinions, brief 'human' stories – anything which will back up your argument.

For instance... To take an example:... This has been forcefully illustrated by the example of...

• USE RHETORICAL QUESTIONS TO REINFORCE YOUR POINTS.

A rhetorical question is one which does not expect an answer. Its purpose is to reader the reader or listener thinking.

Are we really being asked to believe...? But is this the only possibility...? What would happen if...?

Take your reader with you.

• USE A TOUCH OF HUMOUR.

It is good to make your readers smile occasionally; it helps to get them on your side.

• ANTICIPATE COUNTER ARGUMENTS

People are often resistant to a new approach, so be ready defend it against possible objections.

Perhaps we need a new approach. Why not try....? Although this may prove difficult, I believe it would be possible if...

Anticipate any arguments an opponent may bring forward, and deal with them. Cheerfully admit any drawbacks in your suggested solution, but state your belief that these can be overcome.

Admittedly, there are certain problems. Some people might argue that... Despite this, however...

• BEFORE CONCLUDING, RE-STATE YOUR CASE

Having explained all your points in turn, dealt with any problems, and made an effective case for your idea, re-state your position clearly and forcefully.

In view of all this... I feel very strongly that... There can be no doubt...

• YOUR CONCLUSION

End on a clear, forceful note. Your last sentence should be punchy and memorable. A short one works best.

Whatever conclusion we may draw from all this, there is no doubt that this problem requires urgent attention. We ignore it at our peril.

FOR PRACTICE
Put together an effective argument for (or against) one of the following:

1. Changing something (meals? the timetable? the rules?) at your school;

2. A change in the whole education system;

3. Banning something you would like to see stopped (hunting? animal experiments?);

4. Allowing something which is illegal at present (euthanasia? smoking cannabis? the death penalty?);

5. Improving the rights and conditions of a section of society (ethnic minorities? refugees? children?) .

You may think of other suitable topics. Choose one about which you feel strongly – and preferably that you also know a little about.

USING PERSUASIVE LANGUAGE

Although you may often find yourself doing both at the same time, there is a distinction between putting forward a straightforward argument, and aiming specifically to **persuade** the reader.

You have already looked at several **persuasive techniques**: rhetorical questions, repetition, humour, giving examples, citing facts and figures, quoting other opinions. Another way to carry your readers with you is to use examples that appeal to their humanity. Make them **feel** sympathy for, say, victims of injustice.

Advertisers, of course, are always trying to persuade us – to buy their products. Politicians also are great persuaders – they want us to accept their policies. It is useful to spot how they do it. They don't just want us to agree; they want us to **feel** a certain way as well. So they use persuasive language.

Persuasive language stirs our emotions. For example, some newspaper favourites:

It's a terrifying thought. ...guilty of cruel and evil behaviour. Unimaginable squalor – ...a horrific scene.

Or, more positively,

...glamorous and sophisticated lifestyle... Scenes of indescribable jubilation... What a wonderful idea! The queen looked magnificent... Unbelievable generosity...

Persuasive language also appeals to our imagination:

Imagine how you would feel if... Put yourself in that poor mother's shoes... Picture the scene... Suppose you heard you had won the lottery... What would you do if...?

FOR PRACTICE

Write a piece appealing in the strongest possible way to your reader's feelings about one of the following topics (or anything else you might feel strongly about):

1. Pollution.
2. Racism.
3. Bullying.
4. Cruelty to children or animals.

INTRODUCTION

A literary essay, as distinct from any other kind of essay, is one in which you discuss some aspect of a work of literature – prose (novel or short story), drama or poetry. The basic principle is the same as for any essay. You are presented with a **question** or topic; in response to it you present a **case**, in the form of a structured **argument**, backed up by **evidence**.

The question may take any number of different forms. For example:

> *What impression do you have of the character A? How does the author convey this impression?*
> *Do you find the ending of the novel ... satisfactory?*
> *Show how the author brings out the suspense in the final scene of the play.*
> *Comment on the theme of ... in the novel/play.*
> *How appropriate do you find the title ... for this play/novel?*
> *Explore the theme of ... in the poetry of ....*
> *Do you find this poem effective? Give your reasons.*

BACK IT UP
In all cases, even if the question does not say so, the most important thing to remember is that you must **SUPPORT** your answer with **EVIDENCE FROM THE TEXT**.

So – how should you proceed?

LOOK CAREFULLY AT THE QUESTION

Decide exactly what is being asked. Jot down your initial response.

e.g. Character of A – loyal, honest, simple-hearted, a bit naive.

READ OVER THE RELEVANT PIECE

Make a brief note as you go along of anything that may be useful for your purpose. (In a longer work, note down the page number where you found a useful passage, so that you can find it again.)

If you are writing about a whole book or play, you will need to **skim-read** (see Study Skills, page 72) in order to find the passages which are relevant to the question. You should anyway know the book well enough, if you have studied it, to recognise which parts may be relevant for your purpose. You may also wish to consult the list of chapter headings, if there is one.

WHAT POINTS AND IN WHAT ORDER

You should by now have a good pile of material to draw upon. Now you need to choose what to use and what to leave out. You also need to decide what would be the best order to follow. (Just chronologically following the order of the story isn't necessarily the best method. Take time to think about an effective way to arrange your ideas.)

HOW LONG SHOULD IT BE?

Your essay will probably cover about FIVE OR SIX MAIN POINTS, each of which will have a whole paragraph, or possibly 2 or 3 paragraphs, to itself.

Make a rough plan: **Point 1:** – x.
                      Point 2: On the other hand – y.
                      Point 3: Another aspect is – z... etc.

GO BACK TO THE ORIGINAL QUESTION.

In the light of your researches, decide what your basic 'case' is going to be. Do you agree with what the question implies? Do you want to say 'partially yes, partially no'? What do you want to say about the opening/ending of the novel/play? Most answers will contain something of the 'on the one hand x, but on the other hand y' variety.

Don't forget, also, that a character may well change over the course of a play or novel, so your final conclusion may be very different from your first impression. Your answer may need to trace the course of the character's development.

It helps always to keep in mind the question – what is the author's attitude; how does he or she want us to feel about this person/event?

WRITE THE TITLE AT THE TOP OF THE PAGE.
This will help you to keep your mind on the question; you'll be less likely to wander off the point.

WRITE YOUR INTRODUCTORY PARAGRAPH

In the opening paragraph you state very simply your attitude to the question. Try to keep it short.

e.g. The theme of … recurs at several different points in this novel. Whether it is the most important theme, however, is open to question.
Or The first impression we receive of B is misleading. At first he seems quite …, but later in the novel it becomes obvious he is really ….
Or All of …'s female characters are …, and C is no exception.

Or whatever may be appropriate.

THEN TAKE EACH OF YOUR POINTS IN ORDER

There is a very definite procedure to be followed here:

State your point.

Show by referring to the text where or when what you are talking about happens.

E.g. *C is very impulsive. For example, when she hears that …, she immediately and without thinking does ….*

If possible, give more than one instance to support your point.

E.g. *Again, when she hears that …, she ….*

You may find there are three of four examples.

Whenever possible, quote from the text to illustrate your point.

E.g. *She is described by B as "… and …".*

Add your own comment.

E.g. *All of this makes us see her as ….*

COVER ALL YOUR POINTS IN THIS WAY

When you have dealt with the first point as fully as you can, move on to your next point, starting a new paragraph and following the same procedure. You should try to link your paragraphs with phrases such as:

Another aspect of A's character is shown in Scene 4, when…….
However, this is not the whole picture.
On the other hand…..
The theme of … occurs again towards the end of …..
All this might suggest …, but if we consider ……..

Continue in this way until all your points are fully covered and your have supported each one of them with appropriate **evidence** and **quotation** from the text.

Then –

WRITE A SHORT CONCLUDING PARAGRAPH

This may sum up what you have been saying, but in any case it should round off your essay.

> *E.g. In the end, we cannot help liking A, despite all his faults, and we are glad when, in the closing pages of the novel, he.......*
> *Or The theme of ... certainly plays a central role in this play. As we have seen, all the characters ...., but in the end it is ... which is truly important. – etc. etc.*

CHECK IT AGAIN
Check for mistakes, and make sure that every sentence a) makes sense, and b) follows on naturally from the one before it.

DON'T FORGET TO LISTEN!

The most important thing, throughout the whole process of writing, is that you **LISTEN TO WHAT YOU ARE WRITING**. For this you have to **concentrate** hard throughout the whole process. Try not to let anything interrupt you. If you are forced to interrupt your writing, make sure that when you come back to it you re-read from the beginning, so as to 'read yourself into it' again, and pick up the overall sound of your essay.

SOME TECHNICAL POINTS

When you refer to the **title** of a novel or play, <u>underline</u> it if you are writing by hand, or put it in *italics* if you are doing it on a computer.

When you quote from the text, put the bit you are quoting within **quotation marks**. If you quote someone else's opinion (for example, a literary critic's), again put it within quotations marks, and put the person's name in brackets after it. (You can, if you prefer, add a footnote instead. (To make a footnote, put an asterisk (*), or a small number (^{2}) if you need more than one footnote, after the quotation, and another asterisk or number at the bottom of the page or at the end of your essay, and add the footnote beside it.)

Try to **incorporate quotations into your own writing** smoothly, so that the whole makes sense. For example:

> *The author describes C as '... ...' and this is borne out when she... Or: What B says next is interesting: '"...,' she said quietly, trying not to show her emotions.' Clearly, she feels ...*

Always **quote enough for the reader to understand** what you are talking about. Don't leave incomplete phrases hanging.

You should **always write in the present tense** in a literary essay.

*D **is** a complex character* (not: was). *He **acts** strangely* (not acted). *The next day, he **arrives*** (not: arrived) *at the house…*

DO NOT JUST RE-TELL THE STORY!

Your job is to **analyse** and **comment**. You should refer to and/or quote just those parts of the story that you need to make your point and illustrate it. Inexperienced writers all too often get carried away with telling the story, and forget all about the question they are meant to be answering. So keep checking that you are still on track!

FOR PRACTICE

Next time your teacher asks you to write about a story, a novel, a play, or poetry – try following the instructions given in this section. Alternatively, you might like to write an analytical essay about one of your favourite books.

(You will find some special hints on writing about poetry on the next page.)

WRITING ABOUT POETRY

INTRODUCTION

Writing about poetry is like putting the poem or poems under a magnifying glass to examine them closely, and then describing what you see. It is really very simple, although people often seem to think it is something difficult. But you do need, just as you would if you were describing, say, a biological specimen, to know how to use certain technical terms. We call these 'literary terms'. You will find most of the ones you will need, and any that are mentioned in this section, explained on page 63.

FIRST, READ THE POEM!

This sounds obvious, but it is surprising how some people try to write about a poem before they have really read it properly. Read it slowly, out loud. Hear it. Listen to the rhythm and sound of it. Let it really speak to you, even if you don't understand it at first. If there are any words you don't understand, look them up, or ask someone.

SOME QUESTIONS TO ASK YOURSELF

WHAT IS THE POEM ABOUT?

What is its theme? What is the poet saying about his or her subject? What is the poet's attitude? What does he or she intend the reader to feel or understand ?

To whom is the poem addressed? Is it a 'private' poem, dealing the with poet's personal thoughts and feelings? Is it an 'observation' poem, describing something the poet has seen, heard or experienced? Is it a 'public' poem, dealing with some great event, or with social conditions, perhaps? Is it a love poem?

Who is the 'speaker' in the poem? Is it the poet, or someone else? Does the poem tell a story? Does it present an argument, or the working out of an idea?

WHAT IS THE TONE OR MOOD?

How does it make you feel? Is it a happy poem, a sad poem, a funny poem? Are the tone and mood the same throughout, or do they change? How are they conveyed? What is the poet feeling?

WHY USE THESE WORDS?

Look at the poet's choice of words and phrases. What effect do they have? Do any words or phrases stand out as especially effective, or emotionally powerful, or unusual?

WHAT ABOUT THE RHYTHM?

Is there variation in the pace and rhythm? If the lines are slow and long drawn out, what makes this happen? If they are fast and light-footed, how does the poet achieve this? Do the poem's pace and rhythm reflect its mood and meaning?

DOES THE POET USE IMAGERY?

Does the poem contain any similes or metaphors? (Sometime the whole poem is a metaphor.) Does the poem create a mental picture in your mind? How does the poet use the senses – sight, hearing, touch, taste, smell?

OTHER POETIC TECHNIQUES?

Does the poet use **repetition** – of single words, phrases, whole lines? If so, what does this do? Is there **alliteration**, or **assonance**, or **onomatopoeia**? If so, what effect does this have? Listen carefully to the sound of the words? Does the sound help the meaning? Are there strong **contrasts** in the poem? What about **questions**?

(You should try to comment on the *effect* of literary devices, rather than just mentioning them.)

WHAT IS THE POEM'S STRUCTURE?

Look at the **shape** of the poem. How does it begin, and how does it end? Is there a climax? Is there a progression of some kind through the verses? What about **tenses** – is the poem dealing with the past, the present, the future, or a mixture of these? How does **time** affect the poem's construction? Does the poem present a **question** or **challenge**? If so, does it offer a solution, or leave the question open?

WHAT IS POEM'S FORM?

How many verses (or *stanzas*) are there? How many lines to each? How long are the lines? Is there a regular pattern? Is there a rhyme scheme? Is there a regular rhythm?

NOW YOU ARE READY TO BEGIN WRITING!

Once you have thought about all these questions, you are ready to write about the poem This is the part that some people find a little tricky. So here, to help you, are some suggested phrases you may find useful.

• OPENINGS

This is a poem about....In this poem, Smith explores/deals with/presents a number of ideas.....This poem is, in effect, a conversation/question/series of questions/narrative about/an argument.....

• GENERAL POINTS

In the first stanza/verse....(second/third, penultimate, final). The first three stanzas/six lines.....deal with/describe....The poem begins by.....The poet then turns his or her attention to.....Finally, the reader is reminded of.....

• SPECIFIC POINTS

The reference to '[quotation]' reminds us of/recalls/suggests...The word '[quotation]' in the first stanza anticipates/echoes/is picked up by/is echoed by the word/phrase '[quotation]' in stanza 4. The word/phrase '[quotation]' in line 3 gives a sense of/has the effect of/makes us feel that.....

The use of alliteration in line 10 – '[quotation]' – suggests/adds to the feeling of/gives an impression of....The alliterating t's, and d's/dental sounds..../the repetition of the liquid sounding l's and w's.../the soft, alliterated sibilants/s's reinforce the sense of.....

The words/lines '[quotation]' have an onomatopoeic effect; they sound like..../they suggest...The onomatopoeic phrase '[quotation]' in line 2, which is repeated in a slightly different way in line 9, reinforces the poem's mood of...../further stresses the poet's feeling of..../gives the reader a sense of...There is a hint of......in lines .....

The imagery in verse 6 is closely related to....The poet uses the metaphor of.....to suggest the idea of.....The sensory imagery in verse 3 is especially effective. Smith uses the image of....to convey. The simile in line 14 – 'like [quotation]' – is particularly apt/vivid/surprising/delightful.

The poet refers to the senses/time/the elements throughout the first half of the poem. The mood/tone changes at line 7, with the introduction of....The pace of these two lines is slow and measured/faster/suggests a dance/the slow movement of.....The rhythm speeds up/slows down with the words '[quotation]'.

• ROUNDING OFF POINTS

The overall tone/mood of the poem is one of ....The mood changes from one of......to ....The poet leaves us with a feeling of...../a question/the sense that....The poem ends where it began, with the repetition of the first line, but with a subtle difference....There is a sense of finality/resolution/despair/hope (etc.) in the final two lines. The poem ends on a note of......

VARYING YOUR EXPRESSION
Here are some words and phrases which may help you to write about literature in general.

WORDS OR PHRASES MAY:
convey, suggest, give a sense of, give a feeling of, impart, communicate, express, assert, speak of, breathe of, remind us of, describe, infer, imply, get across, refer to, drive at, allude to, mean, signify, hint at, paint a picture of, give an impression of, draw attention to, transmit, signal, whisper, declare...etc.

For further variation, you can turn most of the above into the passive mode – e.g. is conveyed by, is suggested by, etc.

DON'T SAY 'IT SAYS'
• **At all costs AVOID saying** "it talks about" or "it says".
• Use the author's **surname** (*not* his or her first name!), or 'the writer', 'the poet', 'the author'; or you can say 'the poem/novel/passage/line refers to...'

FOR PRACTICE
Take any fairly short poem that you have enjoyed and write as much as you can about it using the suggestions given above.

INTRODUCTION

These are the names we give to **literary devices** – methods used by writers and poets to make their writing more effective and vivid.

IMAGERY

creates vivid pictures or sensations in the mind by likening one thing to another; it includes metaphors and similes. (A poem may be an extended image or set of images.)

A SIMILE

brings out a point of likeness or comparison between two different things. It is usually introduced by the words *like* or *as*.

> Her face was *as white as a sheet*.
> My love is *as a red, red rose*.
> My knees were *like jelly*.
> Speed bonny boat, *like a bird on the wing*.

A METAPHOR

is a condensed simile (without the words *like* or *as*). One thing is said to be the other thing with which it is compared.

> Your mother is **an** *angel*.
> There is a *mountain* of work to do.
> Human life is *a journey*.

PERSONIFICATION

is treating an abstract quality (like Justice or Honour or Time) as if it were human:

> *Death hovered near his bed.*
> *Fear stalked the streets.*
> *Luck, be a lady tonight.*

It is also commonly used to endow non-human things with human feelings:

> *The house waited patiently for its owner's return.*

Ascribing human feelings to Nature is called **pathetic fallacy** (pathetic here means 'to do with feelings'):

> *The angry winds, the cruel frost, the kindly sun.*

A SYMBOL

is an object (or set of objects) standing for some idea. For example:

The cross is a symbol of Christianity.
The crown and sceptre are symbols of royalty.
The dove is a symbol of peace.

AN ALLEGORY

is a story which carries another and deeper meaning; the story stands for or suggests something else. For example:

the poem *The Ancient Mariner* is an allegory about guilt.
Pilgrim's Progress is an allegory of the spiritual life.
Animal Farm is a political allegory.

A PUN

is a play on words, usually on two meanings of the same word:

Drilling holes is boring.

HYPERBOLE

is exaggeration for effect:

This skirt is miles too long.
I could eat an ox!
I've told you a million times....

A PARADOX

is a saying which seems to contradict itself; its apparent nonsense, however, emphasises a truth.

More haste, less speed.
What you try to keep for yourself, you lose; what you give to others, that becomes your own.

A EUPHEMISM

is a mild or indirect way of describing an unpleasant or embarrassing thing:

My wife has passed away.
They are sleeping together.
Could I use your smallest room?

IRONY. There are two main kinds:

• **VERBAL IRONY** – when you mean the opposite of what the words state:

> *We've run out of milk? Great...*
> *'For Brutus is an honourable man;*
> *So are they all, all honourable men.'*
> *(Antony in Julius Caesar)*

• **DRAMATIC IRONY** – when the reader or audience knows something that one or all of the characters on stage or in the story don't know. For example, in Jane Austen's novel *Emma*, the heroine, Emma, thinks that the creepily dreadful Mr Elton is in love with her friend Harriet. The reader knows that in fact it is Emma herself that he is after. So we watch in amusement as, because of this error, Emma keeps making disastrous mistakes.

ONOMATOPOEIA

is using words which, through their own sound, imitate or suggest the sound of what they describe:
> *miaow, buzz, crash; the crunch of gravel; the hiss of a steam engine.*

ALLITERATION

is the repeating of sounds (usually consonants at the beginning of words) to echo the sense or sound of the thing described:

> *The stuttering rifle's rapid rattle. Fair stood the wind for France.*
> *Over the foaming flood, the ship sped steadily onward.*

ASSONANCE

is repeating vowel sounds used for a similar purpose to alliteration:

> *and green and deep*
> *The stream mysterious glides beneath,*
> *Green as a dream and deep as death.*
> *(from Grantchester, by Rupert Brooke)*

OXYMORON

is the combination in one expression of two words or phrases of opposite meaning, for effect.:

> *'Idiot savant; false truth; ugly beauty.*
> *Why then, O brawling love! O loving hate!'*
> *(Romeo and Juliet)*

INTRODUCTION

Sometimes – if you're lucky! – you may be asked to write your thoughts about a rather different kind of subject – something that goes a little deeper than usual. (For example, 'Freedom', or 'Friendship', or 'Death', or 'Silence', or even 'God'.) You may in any case want to do this for yourself. There is no better way to sort your own ideas out than to sit down and write about them.

WHAT DO YOU THINK?

What kind of things have you thought deeply about? What 'life questions' do you have? What conclusions have you come to? Or have you perhaps simply found yourself led on to ask further questions?

TRY OUT YOUR OWN POWER OF THOUGHT

It is natural for human beings to want to think and question, to wonder about the 'big' questions. If we didn't do that, we'd be little better than robots. It also happens to be a deeply satisfying thing to do. So try it. You'll be surprised what it can show you. This is what 'reflection' means – it is holding up a mirror so that you can see yourself and the world more clearly.

FOR PRACTICE

Choose a subject that you would enjoy thinking deeply about. It should not be the kind of thing you can learn about from books. Take something more abstract, such as the topics mentioned in the first paragraph, for which you have to look inside yourself. Write about it. Allow your thoughts to flow freely, and don't stop until you feel you have written everything that's there in your mind to be said about it.

ANYTHING GOES

There is no particular way to do this. Just spend a little time thinking about the topic. Make an essay plan if it helps you. Then just start writing. Take your mind for a walk. See what you discover.

You may like to read the essay on page 67 so as to get the general idea of writing reflectively.

THE PLEASURES OF SOLITUDE

There is, up to a point, a certain amount of pleasure derived from being alone, like a hermit in a cell; but a huge cell. A cell as big as the world; and it's yours, and only yours, to explore.

The life I lead is full of people; brimming with brothers, sisters, friends and more. But when I need rest, or when life has really put its yoke on my neck, then I must be alone. I go out into an empty world and watch people in their own lives, and then I know they are happy because they are alone too.

Solitude quietens me down and then brings me totally to my senses, and everything gently simmers down into a pool of freshness.

But many would prefer to rush out and join the throng of life, and collect friends, and take them out into a waiting world of cinemas and throbbing strobe lights.

But no, that life is not for me. The lights just give me headaches, and I see my friends at school.

I like to be alone, where there is nothing to disturb the quiet. Solitude is a chance to open out in the swing of nature. Dark damp forests, lush green grass, splinters of light falling through a country glade, all can be enjoyed, but if you are alone with them, they become part of you. You can feel the way trees feel, swaying in the wind, and you know all you need to know.

The place solitude tugs most at my head, though, is its inner world. There lies complete stillness, like a restful pool of tranquil water in the burning heat of day. And as I lower myself into this 'pool' I feel the pleasures of solitude rush around me, and it is then that I realise, and acknowledge with my full heart, that solitude is not loneliness. For I am not lonely when I am alone and without a fellow companion, and I like it that way.

This does not mean that I do not enjoy my friends' company. Of course I do. But it is solitude I desire most, and I expect it will always be so.

David Story, Age 11

STUDY SKILLS

INTRODUCTION

This section shows you how to make the best use of dictionaries and other reference books, that can be of help to a writer.

USING YOUR DICTIONARY

A good dictionary contains a wealth of information. Yours should be your constant companion, something you keep with you and turn to just about every day. What can it tell you? More than you might think.

• SPELLING

This is the most obvious thing. Your dictionary is arranged in **alphabetical order**. That means that if you want to look up a word like, say, *consternation* (well, you might!), you open the dictionary near the beginning, at *c*. Then you look at the top of the page where the first and last word on that page are written. You want *co* – so turn the pages until you find words beginning with *co*; then *con*. There'll be lots of words, include 'con' itself, that begin con. Turn on till you find *cons-*, then *const-* and you're there.

• MEANING.

Meanings are very interesting. Look carefully at all the meanings given for the word. But bear in mind that no two words have exactly the same meaning. There will be a subtle difference between the meaning of the word you have looked up, and the meaning the dictionary offers. For example, one dictionary gives, under *consternation*, the meaning 'amazement'. But they are not at all the same thing. Amazement can be joyful, full of wonder. Consternation suggests alarm, fear, shock. So it's a particular kind of amazement.

Many words have several totally different meanings. Try looking up the word tender, for instance. Three quite different meanings spread readily to mind – can you find them? Or try the word *fast*.

• PART OF SPEECH

Your dictionary will also tell you whether a word is a noun, verb, adjective, etc. This information is usually given in brackets after the word, and often abbreviated to *n., vb., adj., prep.* (You will find a list of abbreviations that your dictionary uses at the front of it.) Many words have different meanings as different parts of speech. Look up the word round, for example. It means different things as a noun, a verb, an adjective and a preposition.

• STRESS

When a word has more than one syllable, it will have a stress on one of them, which means you pronounce that syllable more strongly than the others. The word *display* has the stress on the second syllable. The word *second* has it on the first. (There is another meaning of *second*, meaning 'transfer to other duties' where the stress falls on the second syllable.) Your dictionary should show you where the stress comes, either by printing it in bold letters (tre-**men**-dous), or by putting a colon or accent mark of some kind before it (tre´mendous; tre:mendous). There are many words in English which have a different stress depending on the word is being used as a noun or a verb. For example: *contract, dictate, contrast, convert, digest.*

Some dictionaries also give you the correct pronunciation. For example, you might find:

> *legion* (**lee**-jon), *n.*
> *legislate* (**lej**-iss-layt) *vb.*

• ORIGIN

This is in some ways the most interesting part. An etymological dictionary (Greek *étumos*, true, *étumon*, the literal sense of a word + *logos*, word) will tell you what language the word originally came from, and what its component parts mean in that language, when it first entered the English language, and, if you're lucky, some of its history since then. One favourite is our old friend, the word *nice* – the one your teacher has probably told you not to over-use. Here's its history.

Nice
Nice comes from Latin *nescius*, ignorant, from *ne* (not) + *scire*, to know. It came into English from Old French (where it meant 'silly' or 'simple') in the 13th century, when it meant 'foolish, stupid'. In the 14th century it came to mean 'wanton'; in the 15th, 'coy', 'shy'; then, in the 16th it took on the meanings of 'fastidious, dainty'; 'difficult to manage'; 'minute and subtle'; 'precise, critical'; 'minutely accurate'. (It can still have this meaning today, as in 'a nice distinction') Finally, in the 18th century it arrived at the meaning we mostly use today: 'agreeable, delightful'.

THE BEST YOU CAN GET
So get yourself the best dictionary you can. And give yourself a treat by going to your local reference library and taking a look at the grandfather of all dictionaries, the huge, twelve-volume *Oxford English Dictionary*, accepted the world over as the authority on words, and known affectionately to all word-lovers as the *OED*.

USING A THESAURUS

Use a thesaurus (Greek *thesauros*, treasure) to help you find the exact word, the exact subtle shade of meaning you want.

You know those occasions when a word doesn't seem quite right for what you are trying to express? Or when you feel the right word is just on the tip of your tongue but you just can't remember it? That's when you turn to your thesaurus. Or maybe you have used the same word too often in a piece of writing, and you want to vary it. Look it up in your thesaurus, and you should find a whole list of suggested alternatives.

Roget's Thesaurus is the best known one, but there are many alternative editions available now. Have a look in the reference section of your local bookshop. There is also a 'thesaurus' among the 'tools' – along with spell-check, word count etc. – on the desktop of a computer, but these are seldom as full – or as much fun – as a proper thesaurus.

LOOKING UP A WORD

The thesaurus is divided into two sections: an **index** section, and a **reference** section. Start with the index, which is arranged in alphabetical order, and look up the word which is nearest to the one you are looking for, or for which you want to find an equivalent. Underneath that word, you will find one or more alternative meanings – what it means as a noun, what it means as a verb, and so on – each with a reference number.

So – if you look up the word *amazement* in the index, you find, underneath it: *inexpectation 508 n.* and *wonder 864 n.*

If you're more interested in the sense of amazement meaning 'surprise', you will turn to section 508 in the reference section. Here you find the word *Inexpectation*, followed by, under N for noun, a series of words which don't seem very helpful. But as you read on down the list you come to:

> *surprise, surprise packet, Jack-in-the-box, shock, start, jolt, turn, blow; bolt from the blue; thunderclap, bombshell; revelation, eye-opener; paradox, reversal, peripeteia; amazement.*

Perhaps one of these is what you want.

If, on the other hand, the meaning you want is closer to wonder, then you will turn to section 864 in the reference section, where you will find, under Wonder, N, the words

> *wonderment, admiration, hero-worship, awe, shock, astoundment, amazement, stupor, stupefaction.*

None of these seem quite right, so you follow on down the entry to find

> *phenomenon, miracle, sign, marvel, wonder; drama, sensation, fairy-land, fantasy...*

Aha — *miracle* — that's what you want. Or perhaps *marvel...* So you try these words out in my sentence, to see which of them feels just right.

CHOOSE YOUR WORDS WELL

Always be very choosy about the words you use. Be 'nice' (in the sixteenth-century sense) about them. Don't be content until you have captured just the word you want. Use your dictionary and thesaurus to make sure you can.

Use reference books as much as you can. Get into the habit of it. Educate yourself! It's fun!

For other types of reference book and sources of information, see Informative Writing, page 36.

INTRODUCTION

During your English studies you will be confronted with lots of information which you will have to remember. But don't panic – here are a few, easy-to-learn techniques to help you manage it all.

NOTE-TAKING

Any student needs to know how to do this efficiently. Whether you are listening to a talk or lesson, or taking notes from a book, you need to put down the information in such a way that you will easily be able to make sense of it later.

- Take down just the essentials.
- Use as few words as possible – just sufficient to jog your memory. Leave out all but the key words.
- Note brief examples where appropriate.
- Abbreviate long words.
- Divide and rule. Divide the material into sets and sub-sets, listing points and numbering them, using letters, numbers and Roman numerals to help you.
- Note page numbers in the book you are consulting.
- Keep all your notes looking neat and attractive

Notes on this list of points might look something like this:

1. Just essentials.
2. Few words as poss. Key words.
3. Brief eg.s
4. Abbreviate
5. Divide points. Use nos. & letters.
6. Note page nos.

SKIM-READING

You can skim read at different speeds. One method is to turn rapidly over the pages, one by one, without reading anything. Put in a 'half-sticky' or 'post-it note' at the start of each chapter or other significant point. Note chapter headings if the book has them. You can write a couple of words on the post-it note to remind yourself why you put it there.

With slightly slower skim-reading – for example when you are looking for material about a particular aspect of the book – you run your eyes down each page without actually reading the words, but slowly enough so that your eyes pick up anything relevant to your search. When you find something, put in your 'half-sticky'. Then you can come back later and read over the passage more carefully.

MAKING A SUMMARY

If you are **summarising a play or a novel**, make a note for each chapter or scene of the following:

- What happens in that chapter/scene
- Any new character introduced
- Main qualities of the character
- Any change or development of a character
- Any important turning point or climax in the plot

Make a separate note of any comments about the chapter or scene (such as how a theme is developing) that you feel are relevant.

If you have been asked to **summarise a passage of writing**, you should try to:

- include all essential points
- put them as briefly and neatly as possible
- be accurate
- use your own words as much as you can

You should **not**, however:

- give your own opinions
- include examples
- add anything
- use quotations from the passage

PLANNING AND DRAFTING

For help with planning essays and stories, read Writing Essays on page 41, and the notes on plot structure on pages 17. For literary essays, read the relevant sections on pages 54-58.

Once you have a plan, with your ideas arranged in logical order, and the notes from which you will draw your material all prepared, you can begin to write your **first draft**. Note that this **does** not mean 'rough' draft. Your first draft should be as carefully written as anything else.

What it does mean is that you know this is not necessarily going to be the final version, so you don't have to agonise over it too much. For example, many people find it hard to get started. If you're one of those, just decide that you are going to scrap your first paragraph and rewrite it later in any case. So just write anything to get you started, and then you'll find it easier to move on. Come back at the end to re-do the introduction.

LET IT BREATHE
Once you have finished your first draft, if time allows put it away for a week or so. Then come back and re-read it. You will probably immediately see all sorts of things you want to change. Perhaps you could have put these two paragraphs the other way round; you have thought of a much neater way to put this sentence; you have decided to change the ending... If you are a truly skilled writer (and there's no excuse not to be) you will go on improving and perfecting your work until you are completely satisfied that it's as good as it possibly could be. Never hesitate to throw out anything that doesn't seem right.

PRESENT IT BEAUTIFULLY

When you have completed this process – by which time your original draft probably looks a real mess – then, and only then, write or type it up in 'best', presenting it with as much loving care as you can. After all, it's your baby. So take a pride in showing it to the best advantage.

REVISING FOR EXAMS

One of the questions students most frequently ask is 'How do I revise for exams?'

This is where all those careful notes you took come in handy. What you should aim to do is **get an overview** of the subject, or the parts of it that you are going to be examined on. So you want to **reduce it** to manageable 'chunks', and lay it all out so that your mind can 'see' the whole of it.

- Divide the subject into topics – each with a clear heading
- Divide these into sub-topics
- Put all of this onto a single A4 sheet, so that you can see it all at once
- Have an A4 sheet for each topic and sub-topic, which contains in the briefest possible form everything you need to know about that topic.
- Once you have created your revision page, laid out as clearly as can be, don't change it. Let your mind mentally 'photograph' the page.
- Look at your sheets every day. Make sure you have understood their contents. Learn them.

REVISING FOR THE LITERATURE EXAM

Obviously, you need to re-read the text. But also look again at your summary – or make one, if you haven't already. (It's best to make your own, rather than rely on any published "Notes".) Get to know the book inside out and backwards. Re-read any essays you wrote about it. See if you could improve them.

Copy out and **learn** any useful quotations you may want to use in the exam. Don't make these too long – two lines at the most, or you won't remember them. It's worth learning your quotations even if you are going to be allowed to have the book with you in the exam. You won't have time to fish around looking for them.

IN THE EXAM

- READ THE QUESTION! You would be amazed how many people fail to do that simple thing. Make sure you are absolutely clear what you are being asked to do.

- Read over all the questions before you start. That way you'll avoid unnecessarily overlapping your answers.

- If the exam consists of essay questions, do the one you feel happiest about first.

- If there is a choice of essay questions, decide which ones you are going to do before you start the first one. You will find that your brain has been quietly busy while you were writing the first answer getting the second one prepared. Goodness knows how it does this, but I assure you it does!

- Take great care over your first sentence and your first paragraph. Make a good impression.

- Work as swiftly as you can. Time yourself carefully. Don't be tempted to spend longer than you should on any question. You will only run yourself out of time later, and lose marks.

- Always leave enough time to check over your work for spellings, words left out, punctuation, or sentences that don't work. Make corrections neatly.

HINT!!

INTRODUCTION

This section is about the nuts and bolts of language; about taking language apart to see how it is made. But as you'll know if you have ever taken anything to pieces, it is equally important to be able to put it back together in the right order so that it will work. That is what this thing called 'Grammar' is all about – taking language apart, having a good look at it, and then putting it back together.

There is a beautiful order and harmony in the way that language works, building up from the smallest and simplest unit to the largest and most complex. Sounds and letters combine to form words; words divide into different classes according to the work they do; they in turn combine to form phrases, clauses and sentences, performing different functions within those larger units. Sentences combine to form whole paragraphs. And paragraphs are brought together to create novels, short stories, plays, poems, articles, reports, letters, diaries, histories, biographies – and books on every subject under the sun!

One of the advantages of learning about the basic grammatical structure which underlies language is that it is essentially the same for all languages throughout the world. So in mastering English grammar you are well on the way to understanding any other language you may choose to learn…

You have probably already learnt a good deal about all this, but whenever you are not quite sure about a point of grammar or punctuation you may find it useful to turn to this section and check it out.

A word about how this section is arranged: the different topics have been arranged into a clear and logical sequence. After each main topic, there is a 'Test Yourself' section – exercises to help you check that you have understood the topic. You will also find the occasional 'Error Alert' to help you avoid common mistakes.

The topics are broken down as follows:

The basic elements: letters, syllables, words.
Parts of Speech: nouns, verbs, pronouns, adjectives, adverbs, conjunctions, prepositions, interjections.
Word building: prefixes and suffixes.
Parts of sentence: subject, agent, object, indirect object, complement.
Taking a closer look at verbs: different verb forms, tenses and their meanings, non-finite verbs.
Nouns, pronouns, adjectives: a few details.
Sentence building: phrases, clauses: different kinds; types of sentence; identifying the main clause.
Text building: paragraphs, order and structure.
Punctuation: the rules!

THE BASIC ELEMENTS

INTRODUCTION

We begin by looking at the simplest elements of language. It all begins with sound. All of us go through the same process, from the first cry that we make as a new-born baby, going on gradually to acquire the ability to make all the sounds of the alphabet, then to speak words, then to make sentences – until, hey presto, before you know it you are writing whole books, making learned speeches, and who knows what else.

SOUNDS AND LETTERS

These are the most basic elements of language. There are two kinds of sounds: vowels and consonants.

In English there are over twenty different vowel **sounds**, but only five letters to represent them: *a*, *e*, *i*, *o* and *u*. (This is what makes English spelling tricky, especially for foreigners!)

Then we have 21 *consonant letters* – *b*, *c*, *d*, *f* and so on, and we use some of these in pairs – such as *ch*, *th*, *sh* – to represent sounds we don't have single letters for.

WORDS AND SYLLABLES

Sounds and letters combine to form syllables, which combine to form whole words. In English there are many words of **one syllable** – that is, with just **one vowel sound**: *cat, dog, ship, bridge, heap.* (Notice, there may be more than one vowel *letter*.) But words may have **several syllables**. If you speak these words out loud, you will notice they have a 'beat' for each syllable. Try counting them:

> *in-di-gest-ion (4),*
> *el-eph-ant (3),*
> *dict-ion-ar-y (4),*
> *in-def-at-ig-ab-le (6).*

WHAT IS A WORD?

Words are not made up of just any old sounds, and not all combinations of letters make proper words. *Fdrogl*, for example, isn't a word – nor is *klertwa*. At least not in English. Why not? Because they don't mean anything. Even syllables like *-tion* or *-ment* or *un-* are not words, because they don't have any meaning on their own.

A WORD IS AN ARRANGEMENT OF SOUNDS OR LETTERS THAT CONVEYS INDEPENDENT MEANING.

INTRODUCTION

Just as we all play different parts in life (like brother, sister, daughter, son, friend, pupil, etc.), so words in a sentence have different roles to play. There are eight different functions, or jobs, that words have to do. We call these **Parts of Speech (or word classes)**. Here they are:

NOUNS

A NOUN IS THE NAME OF A PERSON, PLACE OR THING, OR OF A QUALITY OR IDEA.

names of people: *Peter, Mr Black, Chief Bigfoot*
names of places: *London, Africa, Heron House, Australia*
names of things: *book, chair, star, water, lamp, computer*
names of qualities or ideas: *truth, beauty, justice, decision, nationality, realisation, coincidence, fear, hope.*

VERBS

A VERB EXPRESSES AN ACTIVITY OR A STATE OF BEING.

actions ('doing' words): *run, laugh, cry, calculate, think, write*
verbs of being: *be, am, is, was, were, become, seem*

(**Tip:** People often forget that words like *is, were* etc. are verbs, because they have been told that verbs are 'doing' words. Remember also that verbs use **auxiliaries**, such as *will, have, had*, etc. to form different tenses – see page 91 – which are also part of the verb)

PRONOUNS

A PRONOUN IS A NAME STANDING IN PLACE OF A NOUN.

personal pronouns: *he, she, it, you, they, me, us, them*
reflexive pronouns: *himself, herself, itself, yourself, yourselves, themselves*
possessive pronouns: *his, hers, its, mine, yours, ours, theirs*
relative pronouns: *who, whom, whose, which, that*
interrogative pronouns: *who? whom? whose? what? which?*
demonstrative pronouns: *this, that, these, those*
indefinite pronouns: *anyone, anything, anybody, no-one, nobody, nothing, everything, everybody, everyone, someone, somebody, something.*

ADJECTIVES

AN ADJECTIVE DESCRIBES A NOUN OR PRONOUN.

adjectives of quality: *happy* man, *blue* sky, *quiet* street
adjectives of quantity: *twenty* pounds, the *first* time; *many* people
possessive adjectives: *my* desk, *your* car, *her* book, *its* fur, *their* work
demonstrative (pointing out) adjectives: *this* house, *that* idea,
                                      these people, *those* thoughts.
interrogative (questioning) adjectives: *which* hat? *what* experience?
                                       whose name?

ADVERBS

AN ADVERB DESCRIBES OR MODIFIES A VERB.

adverbs of manner (how): he spoke *kindly*; she ate *slowly*;
                       they moved *quickly*.
adverbs of time (when): she died *yesterday*; they will arrive *soon*;
                    stop *now*.
adverbs of place (where): It belongs *here*; he ran *away*;
                     she looked *down*.
adverbs of degree (how much): I *nearly* fainted; we *entirely* agree.
interrogative adverbs (questions): *Why* are you late?
                             Where is the station?
                             How does it work?

Adverbs can **also modify adjectives and other adverbs**:

He took a *very* big bite. (*very* modifies the adjective big.)
She walked *fairly* quickly. (*fairly* modifies the adverb quickly.)

Sentence adverbs modify a whole sentence.

However, he did not return.
Obviously, you have not been listening.

CONJUNCTIONS

A CONJUNCTION IS USED TO LINK TOGETHER WORDS, PHRASES OR CLAUSES.

co-ordinating conjunctions (join items of equal status):
         and, but, or, neither ...nor, both ...and, either ...or
subordinating conjunctions (join clauses where one is subordinate to or dependent on the other):
The girl spoke, *although* she was shy. Peter will not come, *because* he is ill. *After* they left, she remembered.

The most common conjunctions are:

after, also, although, and, as, because, before, but, either, for, if, neither, nor, or, since, so, than, though, till, until, unless, when, where, wherever, while.

PREPOSITIONS

A PREPOSITION EXPRESSES THE RELATIONSHIP BETWEEN TWO WORDS OR PARTS OF SENTENCE.
It is followed by a noun or pronoun.

the man *in* the moon; the house *on* the corner;
the lady *with* the hat; keep away *from* him.

Prepositions are used to introduce a prepositional phrase.

near the end; *under* the bridge, *across* the square,
through hard work, *with* us, *before* morning.

The most common prepositions are:

about, above, across, after, against, along, among, around, as, at, below, before, behind, beneath, beside, between, beyond, by, down, during, except, for, from, in, inside, into, like, near, of, off, on, onto, out, outside, over, past, regarding, since, through, toward, towards, under, until, up, with, without.

INTERJECTIONS

AN INTERJECTION IS AN EXCLAMATORY WORD USED TO EXPRESS SURPRISE OR STRONG EMOTION.

help! ouch! Oh no! Yes! wow! bother!

PARTS OF SPEECH

1. Underline the **NOUNS** in this sentence:

   As he stood at the window and watched his father's car turning into Cambridge Road, for the first time in months James felt rising in his heart a certain degree of hope.

2. Underline the **VERBS** (including their auxiliaries) in these sentences:

   After everyone had left, James threw himself down on his bed and began to think. Today had been a nightmare. He was expecting things to go badly, but this was ridiculous. Could he have acted differently, he wondered. If only he had been given more time to think. No doubt his friends would laugh when they heard about it. Well, he said to himself, maybe it will all seem better in the morning.

3. Underline the **PRONOUNS** in these sentences:

   She looked at herself in the mirror and hardly recognised the girl who looked back at her. Nobody would guess it was the same girl who had arrived with everyone else on the coach. They had all looked very sorry for themselves, as it had been a long and exhausting journey, and everyone had just scrambled for their luggage without taking much notice of anyone else. But would he recognise her? She was very afraid of him.

4. Underline the **ADJECTIVES** in the following:

   The small girl picked up her heavy suitcase and began to trudge up the long steep hill. She seemed very young to be alone in this strange, unfriendly city, but it was obviously not the first time she had walked up that hill. It was a hot day and there were few people about. Two or three times the girl stopped to rest for a few minutes before continuing with grim determination.

5. Underline the **ADVERBS** in the following:

   James stared stupidly at the letter. It must have arrived yesterday and had probably been lying there all the time. He had very nearly thrown it away with the rubbish. Fortunately, however, he had hastily checked the papers before he put them in the bin. Now perhaps people would believe he had really told the truth. He went quickly to the telephone.

PARTS OF SPEECH continued

6. Underline the **CONJUNCTIONS** in these sentences.

> He asked if he could speak to Inspector Smith, but was told the Inspector would not be available until tomorrow, as he was busy on another case. James knew that unless he contacted him before Bates arrived, he would have neither the chance to prove his innocence, nor any hope of winning back the trust of his friends. Although some might listen to him, because they respected him, and he knew he could count on Jerry's support, most of them would be influenced by what Mike and Sue had said.

7. Underline the **PREPOSITIONS** in these sentences:

> The little girl walked across the street and sat down on a bench under an acacia tree. She put her suitcase on the ground beside her. From her pocket she pulled a crumpled envelope, and carefully took a letter out of it. Having read the letter, she put it back into her pocket and looked around to see if anyone had followed her. Then she set off again up the street towards the old church.

Answers on page 125.

Don't cheat! Only look them up when you have finished the exercise.

WORD BUILDING

INTRODUCTION

Over the centuries, English has undergone a great deal of change. It has many layers. Each time a new wave of people has come to live in the British isles a new layer has been added, which then blends into the existing language. This helps you to understand when you come to consider how words in English are formed, and how English spelling works.

ANGLO-SAXON

The first 'layer', the original English language, is sometimes called Old English, and sometimes Anglo-Saxon. It gets the name Anglo-Saxon from two of the Germanic tribes, the Angles and the Saxons, who brought it with them when they sailed across the sea, fought the Ancient Britons – who sensibly moved out into Wales and Cornwall – and settled in Britain. They arrived during the 5th century. (The Angles, of course, gave us the names England, and English.) Their language, the first English, is almost unrecognisable to us today, but it gives us all our most basic, simple words – like *earth, sea, sun, moon, child, friend, love, heart.* They are mainly the homely, 'ordinary' words in our language – and also the poetic ones. A great many of them have only one syllable.

THE VIKINGS

The next 'layer' came with the Vikings. Their language was very close to Anglo-Saxon, so they didn't cause much change. We have about 40 Viking words in English today. Some examples: *law, skirt, raise, kirk.* Many place-names are also Viking in origin.

THE NORMANS

When William the Conqueror arrived in Britain in 1066, he and all his barons spoke French. Since they were now the rulers, French became the official language, and everybody had to learn to speak it. Over the next three centuries it gradually blended with the native Anglo-Saxon, adding another 'layer' to produce what is call Middle English – the language of Chaucer and his contemporaries. Over ten thousand French words were adopted into English during this period. Examples of French 'imports': *liberty, infant, nobility, courtesy, gentleness.*

THE RENAISSANCE

During the 16th and 17th centuries, in response to the new ideas and learning from the Italian Renaissance, a further 'layer' was added to English, in the form of learned Latin and Greek words. A huge number of the words in your dictionary come from Latin or Greek. You can usually recognise them because they tend to have several syllables. English took over about a quarter of the Latin words existing at the time. So we have, among countless other examples: from Latin: *significant, expectation, emancipate, extravagant, consider*; from Greek: *autograph, antithesis, catastrophe, phenomenon, enthusiasm.*

THE MODERN WORLD

English has continued to add to its vocabulary from many different sources. Explorers brought back words from Native Americans, from India, China, Africa, Australia. Wars have been another source. And each scientific discovery or new technology brings with it the need for new words. Information technology for example has given our language a host of new terms.

ENGLISH AS A WORLD LANGUAGE

There isn't just one kind of English that is spoken today. English is now the first language in many different countries across the world, and each country tends to develop its own variety of English. American English, for example, is different in many ways from British English. It is also likely that in a fairly short time – perhaps as litle as 50 years – everyone will speak English, at least as a second language.

WORD FORMATION

We have three basic types of word in English. A word which stands on its own and is not combined with any other word or syllable is called a primary word – like *black, white, bird, wash.* A word which is formed by adding together two or more primary words is called a **compound** word – like *blackbird, whitewash.* Or we can take an existing word and add to it a **particle** (that is, a syllable which is not a complete word on its own.) Words formed like this are called **derivative** words.

THE ROOT

The most basic part of a word, which contains its essential and original meaning, is its **root.** Primary words often consist of just the root, and nothing else. For example: *friend, thing, true.* Some, like the word *heart*, which comes from the Sanskirt root *hrid*, can be traced back to a more ancient language.

DERIVATIVE WORDS

These are formed by adding particles to the root. For example:
perspective The root is *spect*, from Latin *specere*, to look.
congratulate The root is *grat*, from Latin *gratus*, pleasing.
enthusiastic The root is *thus*, from Greek *theos*, god.

AFFIXES

These are particles which, as their name suggests, are 'fixed to' or added to a root so as to create a new word. There are two kinds: **prefixes** and **suffixes**.

PREFIXES

These are placed before the root, and are generally used to alter the meaning of the word. Consider: *im-press, ex-press, de-press; in-scribe, de-scribe, sub-scribe, pre-scribe, pro-scribe, circum-scribe*. Here are just a few of the hundred or so prefixes we have in English.

From the old Germanic language (basically Anglo-Saxon) we get:

al-	*al-one, al-most, al-ready, al-together*
mis-	*mis-take, mis-deed, mis-understand*
out-	*out-do, out-shine, out-live*
over-	*over-work, over- eat, over-react*
un-	*un-do, un-wise, un-fair, un-pick*
under-	*under-estimate, under-paid*

From Latin and French:

ad- (to)	*ad-vice, ad-opt, ac-claim, ac-cent, af-fix, ag-gravate, al-lude, an-nex, ap-prove, a-rrest, as-sert, at-tain.*

(Note that when ad- meets a consonant the d often changes to the same letter. The same applies to *con-* and *in-*.)

con- (with)	*con-nect, con-sent, col-lege, com-ment, com-plain, cor-rect, con-sist, con-verge*
ex- (out)	*ex-ample, ex-press, ex-haust*
in- (in)	*in-fect, in-ject, im-migrate, im-part, ir-ritate, in-vite*
in- (not)	*in-elegant, in-firm, il-literate, im-patient, in-nocent, ir-regular, in-sufficient*
per- (through)	*per-form, per-sist, per-haps, per-fect*
trans- (across)	*trans-late, trans-mit, trans-form*

From Greek:

an-a- (not)	*an-archy, a-pathy, a-theist, a-gnostic*
arch- (chief)	*archi-tect, arch-bishop, arch-angel*
auto- (self)	*auto-biography, auto-graph, auto-matic*
dia- (through)	*dia-logue, dia-meter, dia-gnosis, dia-gram*
syn- (with)	*syn-onym, syn-tax, syl-lable, sym-bol, sym-pathy*

SUFFIXES

These are generally used to create a different part of speech. For example, if you take the verb act, you can add *-ion* to form the noun action, *-ive* to form the ajective *active*, and *-ly* to turn that into the adverb *actively*. Here again is just a selection of English suffixes.

To form **nouns**, we use suffixes:

-er, -ar, -or	*help-er, speak-er, li-ar, auth-or, doct-or*
-ant, -ent	*march-ant, tru-ant, ten-ant, stud-ent, cli-ent*
-ist, -ast	*art-ist, botan-ist, cycl-ist, enthusi-ast*
-dom	*king-dom, free-dom, wis-dom, bore-dom*
-ness	*dark-ness, happi-ness, mean-ness*
-ment	*treat-ment, assort-ment, govern-ment*
-age	*cour-age, bond-age, hom-age*
-ance, -ence	*dist-ance, guid-ance, pru-dence*
-ty	*frail-ty, cruel-ty, certain-ty, beau-ty*
-ion	*intent-ion, nat-ion, pass-ion, obliv-ion*

To form **adjectives**, we use suffixes

-ish	*self-ish, wolf-ish, child-ish, slav-ish*
-ant, -ent	*dist-ant, pregn-ant, abs-ent, pres-ent*
-ic	*com-ic, rust-ic, chaot-ic, publ-ic*
-ful	*beauti-ful, plenti-ful, truth-ful*
-ous	*numer-ous, fam-ous, glori-ous*
-ive	*recept-ive, respons-ive, act-ive*
-able, -ible	*not-able, laugh-able, poss-ible, ed-ible*

To form **verbs**, we use suffixes

-en	*sweet-en, enliv-en, length-en, dark-en*
-fy	*terri-fy, electri-fy, glori-fy, intensi-fy*
-ise	*real-ise, terror-ise, brutal-ise, italic-ise*
-ate	*gradu-ate, illustr-ate, demonstr-ate*
-ish	*pun-ish, fin-ish, per-ish, flour-ish*

To form **adverbs**, we use suffixes

-ly	*bad-ly, quck-ly, happi-ly*
-ward(s),	*south-ward, back-ward, to-ward, for-wards*
-ways	*side-ways, length-ways, al-ways*

FOR PRACTICE

Try looking up some of these words in a good etymological dictionary. Discover what their roots mean. Get into the habit of looking at words to see how they are made. You will find this helps you not ony to understand why words are spelt as they are, but also to spell them correctly. Taking words apart into their constituent (that's con-stitu-ent…) parts to discover their deeper meanings can be a wonderfully illuminating exercise. Try it. You may find you develop a fascination for words which stays with you for life.

INTRODUCTION

The section on Parts of Speech showed you how to classify words according to the work they do. Now we shall look at the different functions they perform within a sentence. We call these functions Parts of Sentence.

THE VERB

In order to be a sentence at all, a sentence must have a verb. (In fact it must have a finite verb – you can find out about verbs which 'don't count', because they are non-finite, in Tenses And Their Meanings, page 100) The verb is like the hub of the sentence, round which the other parts revolve. When you are taking a sentence apart to investigate its parts, you always start by looking for the verb.

THE SUBJECT

Every sentence has a **subject**. In a simple way, we could say that the subject is 'the thing we are talking about' – so you would expect it to be the first word of the sentence. And so it is, in most cases. For example: *Dogs bark. Bark* is of course the verb, and *dogs* is the subject. Fine. But because English has an interesting habit of changing the normal word order, things can get more complicated. What about this, for example? *Outside the door stood a tall young man.* The verb is *stood*. But the **subject** is man. *(Or tall young man if we include the describing words.)*

So –

THE SUBJECT IS THE WORD OR WORDS MOST IMMEDIATELY CONNECTED WITH THE VERB.

In most sentences the subject is the 'do-er' of the action.
In the case of the 'being' verbs, the subject is the 'be-er' of the state – the one who is, was, becomes, seems etc..
So to find the subject, look for the verb and ask 'Who or what?'
> *The frog jumped.* (What jumped? – the frog.)
> *She screamed.* (Who screamed? – she.)
> *The audience became restless.* (Who became? – the audience.)

THE AGENT

This is really a more grown-up word for 'do-er' – the one who acts. It is not necessarily, however, the subject of the sentence.

THE AGENT IS THE PERSON OR THING WHICH PERFORMS THE ACTION.

The *captain* ordered the attack. T
The film was directed by *Steven Spielberg*

THE OBJECT

THE OBJECT IS THE PERSON OR THING AFFECTED BY THE ACTION.

The arrow hit *the target*.
Jonathan hates *sausages*.
This will please *her*.
The film was directed by Steven Spielberg.

To find the object, identify the verb and ask 'Who or what is being affected by the action?' – hit what? hates what? will please whom? what was directed?

Notice that in **passive** sentences (such as the fourth example above), the **object of the active verb becomes the subject of the passive verb.**

TRANSITIVE OR INTRANSITIVE VERB?

A sentence only has an object if the verb is a **transitive** one – that is, if the action affects something else: the object. Compare the two sentences below. Both contain the verb *sails*. The first one has an object – *boat*, and the verb is **transitive**. In the second one, there is no object. If you ask 'Sails what?' there is no answer. *Tomorrow* simply tells us when the ship sails. The ship doesn't sail anything. So here the verb *sails* is **intransitive**, and the sentence has no object.

The boy sails his boat.
The ship sails tomorrow.

THE INDIRECT OBJECT

The recipient of the action, the person or thing for whom or to whom an action is done, is called in English grammar the **indirect object**.

THE INDIRECT OBJECT IS THE PERSON OR THING TO OR FOR WHOM THE ACTION IS DIRECTED, OFFERED OR INTENDED.

> I told *Mary* the truth.
> Eve gave *Adam* the apple.
> She is writing *them* a letter.

The verbs are *told*, *gave* and *is writing*. Told what? – told the truth – so *told* is the object. Gave what? – gave the apple – so *apple* is the object. Is writing what? – a letter – so *letter* is the object. But what about *Mary*, *Adam* and *them*? These three are the recipients – the persons towards whom the action is directed. *Mary* is the one who 'receives' the truth; *Adam* 'receives' the apple; the letter is directed to *them*.

THE COMPLEMENT

In sentences where the verb expresses a state of being or becoming, there is no object. Instead we have a complement – the word or words which complete the sense.
(Don't confuse this with the word 'compliment' – something nice said about a person. We are talking about the complement!)

THE COMPLEMENT IS THE WORD OR WORDS WHICH COMPLETE THE SENSE OF VERBS OF BEING AND BECOMING.

> Simon became an *actor*. (*An actor* completes the sense of 'Simon became')
> Berlin is the *capital of Germany*.
> It seems *a shame*.

Note that certain verbs which are normally action verbs can be used to mean 'become' or 'seem'. E.g. *turn, fall, grow, get, look, appear, feel*.

PARTS OF SENTENCE

1. Underline the **SUBJECT** in each of these sentences.

> After a while, the door opened. Out came a shabbily dressed old man. He seemed vaguely familiar to me. Where had I seen him before? Cautiously, I decided to follow him. This, as it turned out, was unwise. The street soon led into an area of town unfamiliar to me. From darkened doorways thin, hungry-looking children stared warily at me.

2. Underline the **OBJECT** in each of these sentences.

> The old man reached the corner surprisingly fast. His daughter, who was watching from the upper window, threw the keys to him. Fumbling in haste, he opened the front door. I cursed my luck. I would not catch him easily now. Still, I might as well take a chance. Nervously, I rang the bell.

3. Underline the **INDIRECT OBJECT** in each of these sentences.

> The child who came to the door gave me a frightened look. Experience had apparently taught her that callers were not to be trusted. I smiled and offered the girl my card. She asked someone behind the door a whispered question. "Please fetch me your mother," I said. She passed the hidden person my request. An older girl put her head round the door and rudely told me to go away.

4. Underline the **COMPLEMENT** in each of these sentences.

> The girl was surprisingly beautiful. But she seemed frightened. I felt ashamed. This was becoming ridiculous. The situation was getting out of hand. Suddenly, it grew much worse. The girl became very angry. She turned white with fury. Then everything fell ominously silent.

Answers on page 125.

Don't cheat! Only look them up when you have finished the exercise.

INTRODUCTION

Unlike the other parts of speech, which mostly stay the same or only change their form from singular to plural, verbs in English take a variety of different forms which you need to understand before you can make sense of the more complex elements of sentence structure.

REMINDER

There are **two basic kinds of verb: 'action' verbs** and **'status' verbs** (or 'doing' and 'being' verbs).

AUXILIARY VERBS

The word *auxiliary* means 'giving help'. Auxiliary verbs 'help' the main verbs to form subtly different meanings. Some of them help to form different **tenses**, some different **moods**, and some are used to give **emphasis**.

> Examples:
> He *reads* the letter (present tense); he *has read* the letter (past tense); he *will read* the letter (future tense).
> I *must try*. You *might succeed*. They *would fail*. (Mood)
> I *do hope*. He *does try*. We *did think*. (Emphasis)

Here is a list of auxiliary verbs:

> Tenses: *be, am, is, are, was, were, being, been, has, have, had, will, shall.*
> Moods: *may, might, could, must, ought to, would, should.*
> Emphasis: *do, does, did.*

> **EACH TO THEIR OWN**
> Sometimes there may be several words between the auxiliary and main verbs.
>> I *have* truly and honestly *searched* everywhere!
>> He *will* very soon *arrive*.
> The verbs here are *have searched* and *will arrive*. You should still consider each as a single verb, even though their parts are separated.

FINITE AND NON-FINITE VERBS

You will have been taught that a sentence must contain a verb. In fact, it must contain a **finite verb**. The word *finite* means 'limited' or 'finished'.

A FINITE VERB IS LIMITED BY PERSON, NUMBER AND TENSE.

Let's consider what this means. (We will look at non-finite verbs later.)

NUMBER

Nouns, pronouns and verbs all change their form according to **number**. That is, depending on whether they are **singular** or **plural.** So we have:

> Nouns: *cat, cats; sky, skies; hoof, hooves; fish, fishes.*
> Pronouns: *I, we; he, they; me, us; himself, themselves.*
> Verbs: *The baby cries. Babies cry. I was angry. They were angry.*

> **MAKE SURE THEY AGREE**
> The verb has to 'agree' with its subject in number – a plural subject must have a plural verb, a singular subject a singular verb. This is why it is incorrect in standard English to say 'He were wrong' (He is singular, so it needs singular verb *was*) or 'They was angry' (*They* is plural, so needs plural *were*).

PERSON

In grammar we speak of three persons: **first person, second person, third person**.

The **first person** is yourself – *I*. In the plural this becomes *we*. A verb is said to be 'in the first person' if its subject is *I* or *we*:
> *I laughed. We were running. I shall begin.*

The **second person** is the person in front of you, the person you are speaking to – *you*. (English used to have the singular pronoun *thou*, but that is now very rarely used.) A verb is said to be 'in the second person' if its subject is *you*:
> *You laughed. You were running. You will begin.*

The **third person** is the person about whom you are speaking – everyone else in the word apart from *I*, *we* and *you*. A verb is said to be 'in the third person' if its subject is *he*, *she*, *it* or *they* – or any noun.
> *He laughed. She was running. It will begin.*
> *They arrived. The car stopped. The man speaks.*

TENSE

The word tense means 'time' (from Latin *tempus*). There are three main tenses, **past, present**, and **future**.

> *I laughed. He ran.* (past tense)
> *I laugh. He runs,* (present tense)
> *I shall laugh. He will run.* (future tense)

But English allows us to make a much more subtle distinction than this. It has seven different tenses. Each of these also has a **simple** and a **continuous** form, allowing even finer shades of meaning.

> *He laughs.* (simple present)
> *He is laughing.* (Continuous present)

There is also an **emphatic** form: *He does laugh.*

You will find a more detailed account of tenses on pages 96-102. But for the moment, see if the statement that **a finite verb is limited by person, number and tense** now makes sense to you. A finite verb must be in first, second or third person (person); it must be either singular or plural (number); and it must be expressed in a particular tense. It can't just float about without being attached to any person or number or tense. Only non-finite verbs can do that.

MOOD

As well as person, number and tense, verbs have four **moods** (or modes) All the tenses may be expressed in any of these moods.

• The **indicative mood**, used when we assert (or deny) anything; this is the normal, familiar use of the verb.

> He *thinks* deeply. I *was* angry. They are *not shouting*.

• The **imperative mood**, used when we command, request or forbid anything.

> *Think* before you speak. Go on – *be* angry.
> *Do not shout.*

• The **interrogative mood**, used to ask questions.
What is he thinking? Are you angry?
Why are they shouting?

• The **subjunctive mood**, used to express a wish, a hope, a doubt or a possibility.

> If he *were to think* more deeply...I wish they were *not shouting*.
> God *save* the King. Heaven *be* praised.

This mood (or mode) of speech is seldom used in modern English, but it survives in phrases such as 'If I were you...' 'Should it prove that...' and 'If only it were so.'

VOICE

English has two 'voices' – active and passive. So we have:

- The **active voice, where the subject is the agent of the action**.
  Shakespeare wrote Hamlet.
  We perfectly understand the rules.

- The **passive voice**, where **the subject is also the object**.
  Hamlet *was written by Shakespeare*.
  The rules are perfectly understood.

Using the passive as opposed to the active voice does not change the meaning; it gives a change of emphasis. It can be used to give a more formal or impersonal effect, as in, say, police statements.

> *The suspect was cautioned and taken to the police station, where he was questioned by two officers.*

Using the passive for 'end focus'

You can also use the passive so as to give more emphasis to a particular word by placing it at the end of the sentence.

> *The mountain rescue team saved my life.*
> *My life was saved by the mountain rescue team.*

The first sentence emphasises the idea 'my life', the second focuses on the idea 'the mountain rescue team'. This is called '**end focus**'; putting a word at the end of the sentence makes the reader focus on it more strongly. Part of the skill of a writer lies in deciding which word or words you want your reader to focus on, and so choosing carefully the most effective order for your sentence. Sometimes a writer will take quite a time trying out different ways of constructing the sentence, before deciding which is the most effective way to write it. You should do the same. Never be satisfied until your sentence sounds and feels exactly 'right'.

UNNECESSARY PASSIVES

You may want to use the passive for a particular effect, but you shouldn't overdo it, or you will just sound pompous. Active verbs give a sense of clarity and vigour.

Compare the following sentences:
> *We need to meet more often.*
> *There is a need for more frequent meetings between us.*

The first sentence is concise, direct and effective. The second sounds weak and flabby.

VERB FORMS

1. Identify the verbs in this sentence, and decide which of the **TWO MAIN KINDS OF VERB** each one is.

> Sarah was a lovely girl. She always had a smile for everyone. I met her last year when we were studying at college. She seemed very happy, and no-one could have guessed anything was wrong. I can't believe this has happened.

2. Supply suitable **AUXILIARY VERBS** in the blanks in these sentences.

> I ....like to know what those two ....doing in my office. They ....been nothing but trouble. I ....send in my report on the incident tomorrow morning. I ....hoped to get away for the weekend, but I ....being prevented by the selfishness of two people who .... behaving disgracefully ever since they arrived.

3. NUMBER: Rewrite the first of these sentences in the plural form (change pronouns as well as nouns and verbs). Then rewrite the second sentence in the singular form.

> **a** I am very pleased to hear that my car is ready, and I will collect it this afternoon.
> **b** The girls say they saw the men helping themselves, but they do not think the men realised they were being watched.

4. PERSON: Rewrite the first sentence in the third person (change pronouns.) Rewrite the second sentence in the first person, and then in the second person.

> **a** My name is Peter, and I am here to talk about myself and the book I have written.
> **b** She is so happy, she hardly knows what to do with herself.

5. MOOD: In which mood are each of these sentences written?

> **a** Please don't make a fuss.
> **c** He is completely innocent.
> **b** How can you say that?
> **d** If only he were!

06. VOICE: In which voice are each of these sentences written?

> **a** The box was carried carefully into the lab and put on the table.
> **b** They opened it up and peered gingerly inside.

Answers on page 125.

Don't cheat! Only look them up when you have finished the exercise.

INTRODUCTION

On page 98 you will find a chart showing all seven of the English tenses with their simple and continuous forms. But first let us look at how the different tenses are used.

PRESENT TENSE

Simple present: *He goes to school.*
Continuous present: *He is going to school.*
Emphatic present: *He does go to school.*

The **simple present** is normally used to describe a habitual action – something which happens often. (He goes to school every day.)
The **continuous present** implies that the action is taking place right now. (He is going to school *now.*)
The **emphatic present** is used to strengthen or emphasise the statement – especially when disagreeing with a previous statement. (He *does* go to school! Did you think he didn't?)

Sometimes the *form* of the present tense may be used to *mean* the future:
The ship sails tomorrow. He is coming back next year .
This really means "The ship will sail tomorrow" and "He will come back next year".

PAST TENSE

Simple past: *I laughed. She spoke.*
Continuous past: *I was laughing. She was speaking.*
Emphatic past: *I did laugh. She did speak.*

The **simple past** tense suggests a single action which happened and finished in the past.
The **continuous past** emphasises the idea of the action continuing and taking a little time: *I laughed while she was speaking.*
The continuous *she was speaking* implies that the action of speaking carried on over a period of time, during which the single action – *I laughed* – took place.

PERFECT TENSE

Simple perfect: *I have run. He has drunk.*
Continuous perfect: *I have been running. He has been drinking.*

The **perfect** tense implies that the action is completed. It generally means a more recent past action than the ordinary past tense.
Consider: *I came to London* – at some unspecified time in the past. *I have come to London* – implies that I have only just come.

PAST PERFECT TENSE (OR PLUPERFECT)

Simple past perfect: *I had finished. You had begun.*
Continuous past perfect: *I had been finishing. You had been beginning.*

The **past perfect** tense is often used to show that one action is finished before another begins – in other words to suggest a sequence: *When he had eaten, he went out.* (Past perfect followed by simple past.)

FUTURE TENSE

Simple future: *They will arrive. It will fail.*
Continuous future: *They will be arriving. He will be seeing you.*

The **continuous future** form often implies that something is happening elsewhere at the time of speaking: *They will be arriving at the theatre by now.*

FUTURE PERFECT TENSE

Simple future perfect: *I shall have heard. He will have seen.*
Continuous future perfect: *I shall have been waiting. They will have been celebrating.*

The **future perfect** tense is used to describe an action which will have been completed at some time in the future: *I shall have heard the results by next week.*

FUTURE IN THE PAST

Simple future in the past: *I would faint.*
Continuous future in the past: *I would be leaving.*

The future in the past tense describes an action which at some time in the past was considered as future: *Last Tuesday, he thought he would resign at the end of the week.*
It generally expresses the idea of an expectation or hope.

TABLE OF ENGLISH VERB TENSES

INDICATIVE MOOD

SINGULAR   PLURAL

SIMPLE	CONTINUOUS	SIMPLE	CONTINUOUS
PRESENT			
I walk You walk (Thou walkest) He/she/it walks	I am walking You are walking (Thou art walking) He/she/it is walking	We walk You walk They walk	We are walking You are walking They are walking
PAST			
I walked You walked He/she/it walked	I was walking You were walking He/she/it was walking	We walked You walked They walked	We were walking You were walking They were walking
PERFECT			
I have walked You have walked He has walked	I have been walking You have been walking She has been walking	We have walked You have walked They have walked	We have been walking You have been walking They have been walking
PAST PERFECT (PLUPERFECT)			
I had walked You had walked She had walked	I had been walking You had been walking He had been walking	We had walked You had walked They had walked	We had been walking You had been walking They had been walking
FUTURE			
I will/shall walk You will walk He/she will walk	I shall be walking You will be walking It will be walking	We shall walk You will walk They will walk	We shall be walking You will be walking They will be walking
FUTURE PERFECT			
I will have walked You will have walked He will have walked	I shall have been walking You will have been walking She will have been walking	We will have walked You will have walked They will have walked	We will have been walking You will have been walking They will have been walking
FUTURE IN THE PAST			
I would walk You would walk She would walk	I would be walking You would be walking He would be walking	We would walk You would walk They would walk	We would be walking You would be walking They would be walking

VERB TENSES

Read the extract below. List all the **VERBS** and identify their **TENSES.** (See how many you can get without looking at the table.)

The young man stared out of the train window, saying nothing. I had been watching him for quite a while. People always interest me, but there was something especially intriguing about this young man's eager face. I had decided I would say something when to my surprise he spoke. "I know you are wondering about me," he said, and I found myself staring into a pair of startlingly blue eyes. "I will tell you all about myself if you like."

"Oh, I wasn't being nosey," I stammered in embarrassment.

"Don't worry," he said, with a disarming smile. "I am going to meet my twin sister – for the first time. I am so excited about it. We were separated at birth you see, and I have been living abroad, so we have never met. I will have been away for ten years come next January. In fact, I didn't even know she existed until a month ago." He stopped and shook his head as if he found his own words hard to believe. "It seems like a miracle," he said, half to himself. "To think that in a few hours I will actually meet her! If anyone had told me that I would find I had a sister, and that today I would be travelling across England to see her – I would have said they were crazy."

"How fascinating!" I said. "No doubt she will have been thinking about you a great deal as well. I wonder what she is feeling."

"I have thought about that a great deal," he said. "I hope she will come to the station by herself to meet me. I want a chance to talk to her alone, before I meet her family. I don't know what she will have told them about me. I don't know how they will react."

I was watching his face. A look of pain had fallen across it. "Why...?" I began, as delicately as I could.

He interrupted me. "We never knew our mother. She gave us away for adoption as soon as we were born," He turned to face the window again. "I am hoping that we can trace her. But I am afraid that this sudden discovery of our hidden past will have come as a great shock to my sister."

Both of us fell silent for a few minutes. then he turned to me again and said, "I can't explain it. But it feels as though I have been living a lie all these years. We will both have been thinking all our lives that we were someone else – we are not who we thought we were. Can you understand that?"

I nodded. Oh I understood all right. Only too well.

Answers on page 126.

NON-FINITE VERBS

There are three kinds of non-finite verb: **infinitive verbs**, **participles**, and **verbal nouns**.

INFINITIVE VERBS

The **infinitive** form of the verb is used to refer to the verb in a general way, without connecting it to a subject. It is expressed with the word *to*, like this:

> To *hope* is vital. I have a lot *to do*. He likes to *give*.

In these examples, it is the **idea** of hoping, doing or giving that is being expressed. But there is no particular person, number or tense attached to *to* hope, *to do*, or *to trave*l.

THE INFINITIVE FORM HAS NO SUBJECT

PARTICIPLES

There are two kinds of participle: the **present participle**, and the **past participle**.

The **present participle** is created by taking the 'stem' of the verb and adding -*ing*. *Hoping, doing, giving.*

It is used in two ways. First, it appears in the continuous form of the verbal tenses: *I am hoping, he was doing, they will be giving* – etc.

Second – and this is the use which concerns us at the moment – it is **used as an adjective**: The *falling* water made a *drumming* sound.

Falling and *drumming* are being used as adjectives, describing the nouns *water* and *sound*. Here are some more examples:

> *Standing* on the corner, he looked up and down the street.
> (*Standing* describes pronoun *he*.)
> *Shouting* as loudly as she could, the girl tried to warn her friend.
> (*Shouting* describes *girl*.)

ERROR ALERT!!
Be careful when you build a sentence beginning, like the last two examples, with a participle. You need to make sure the participle relates to the correct noun or pronoun. Otherwise you end up with a **misrelated, or dangling, participle**. See if you can work out what is wrong with these sentences:
Walking round the corner, the church came into view.
Driving along the coast, the view was fantastic.

No? Well ask yourself when you last saw a church walk – or a view sitting in the driver's seat... This is a very common error – so common that people don't seem to notice it any more. But it's not one that you need ever make!

To correct the two sentences, you would have to say, *'As they walked round the corner...'* and *'As he* [or whichever pronoun is appropriate] *drove along the coast...'*

The **past participle** is usually formed by adding *-ed* to the verb stem. The *locked* door, the *finished* article, a *trusted* friend. Like the present participle, it is used as an adjective, and also to form certain verb tenses: I had *locked*; you have *finished,* she has *trusted*. It is also used to form the passive voice: The door is *locked*. The work was *finished*.

Many past participles do not follow the 'add -ed' rule, but instead change the form of the verb in some other way. Here is a table showing some of the 'irregular' past participles in English.

PRESENT	PAST	PAST PARTICIPLE
tear	tore	torn
sing	sang	sung
break	broke	broken
learn	learned	learnt
run	ran	run
begin	began	begun
wear	wore	worn
write	wrote	written
freeze	froze	frozen
speak	spoke	spoken

You use past participles to form phrases in the same way as present participles. (Remember, they are acting as *adjectives*.)

This coat, *worn* by Lord Nelson, is very valuable.
Sung by the choir, the anthem sounded beautiful.

VERBAL NOUNS

The **verbal noun** (or **gerund**, as it is sometimes called), *looks* exactly the same as a present participle, but instead of acting as an adjective, it is used as a noun.
Smoking is forbidden. *Walking* is excellent exercise.
The only way to tell the difference between a present participle and a verbal noun is to ask – what work is it doing?
The *dancing* leaves. (Participle). She loves *dancing*. (Verbal noun.)

NON-FINITE VERBS

1. In the spaces provided, fill in the **PRESENT PARTICIPLE**, the **PAST TENSE** and the **PAST PARTICIPLE** of these verbs. (The first one has been done for you.)

Verb	Present Participle	Past Tense	Past Participle
drive	driving	drove	driven
find	....	....	....
think	....	....	....
do	....	....	....
weave	....	....	....
cut	....	....	....
ring	....	....	....
take	....	....	....
buy	....	....	....
see	....	....	....

2. Underline the **PARTICIPLES** in the following sentences. Indicate which noun or pronoun each one refers to.

Wailing dismally, the small child held up her broken doll. She looked half frozen. Alice gazed at her, wondering what to do. She bent down, smiling encouragingly, but did not get the expected response. A look of terror darted across the worn little face. Backing away, the child began edging towards the door. Alice, fearing that if found wandering alone at night the little girl might come to real harm, stepped forward, grabbing the child's arm and lifting her bodily from the ground. The child screamed, fighting to get away. Why was she so terrified, Alice wondered. What could have happened to her?

3. Identify the **INFINITIVES** and **VERBAL NOUNS** in the following:

Just talking will not help; we need to act. This is the moment to put our training into practice. The real test is about to begin. And it will not just be about fighting. It is also about understanding your enemy; about being able to wait for the right moment and knowing whether to go in or not.

Answers on page 126.

Don't cheat! Only look them up when you have finished the exercise.

INTRODUCTION

There are still a few details to consider about nouns, pronouns and adjectives. They have certain oddities of behaviour it's useful to know about.

PLURAL NOUNS

Most nouns in English form their plural simply by adding an *s: boy, boys, tree, trees, house, houses* – and so on. But there are several exceptions to this which you should know about. Here they are:

1. Nouns ending in *-s, -sh, -ch, -x,* add *-es. fish, fishes; box, boxes; bus, buses; match, matches, church, churches.*
2. Nouns ending in *-y* **preceded by a consonant change** *-y* to *-ies country, countries; sky, skies; dummy, dummies; duty, duties* – **but** nouns ending in *-y* **preceded by a vowel** just add *-s: toy, toys; donkey, donkeys; jersey, jerseys.*
3. Most nouns ending in *-o* normally just add *-s: solo, solos; piano, pianos.* But *tomato* and *potato* add *-es: tomatoes, potatoes.*
4. Nouns ending in *-is* change to *-es* to form the plural: *crisis, crises; oasis, oases; emphasis, emphases; analysis, analyses.*
5. Nouns ending in *-f* or *-fe* change to *-ves: knife, knives; life, lives, scarf, scarves, thief, thieves; loaf, loaves; self, selves.* Exceptions: *proof, proofs; chief, chiefs; hoof, hoofs* (or – there's a choice – *hooves*).
6. Certain nouns add *-en* to form the plural. *child, children; ox, oxen.*
7. A number of nouns form the plural by changing the middle vowel: *mouse, mice; goose, geese; tooth, teeth; man, men; woman, women; foot, feet; louse, lice.*
8. Certain foreign nouns form their plurals as they did in the languages they originally came from: *phenomenon, phenomena, criterion, criteria, addendum, addenda, memorandum, radius, radii, medium, media*
9. Some nouns have the same form in the singular and the plural: *deer, salmon, trout, sheep, grouse.* (For some reason these are all creatures that people eat or hunt. Interesting…)
10. Some nouns, because of their meaning, have no singular form: *trousers, scissors, mathematics, physics, news, politics.*

POSSESSIVE NOUNS

There are two ways in English to express the idea of 'belonging to' or possession. When speaking, for example of the tail which belongs to the dog, we can say either *the tail of the dog* or *the dogs tail.* To convey the idea 'the lady's hat', 'the book's cover', 'the prisoner's rights' etc. we add an apostrophe plus s to the noun – *lady's, book's, prisoner's* – and then it is called a **possessive noun.**

WHERE SHOULD THE APOSTROPHE GO?

There are four simple rules. Two of them you use all the time; the other two only apply in certain special circumstances.

RULE 1

If the noun is **singular**, the apostrophe goes **before** the s.
The girl's laughter. (Just one girl.) *The baby's face.*

RULE 2.

If the noun is **plural**, the apostrophe goes **after** the s.
The girls' laughter. (Two or more girls.) *The babies' faces.*

These two are very simple and easy to remember. All you have to watch is that you have spelt the plural correctly (see the section on Plural Nouns on page 103).

RULE 3

This rule applies to all the words which do not form their plurals in the regular way by adding -s or -es – such as those listed in numbers 6 and 7 on page 103. Because the words *children, women, men, mice, teeth* etc. are **already plural**, they don't need an s. So you just **treat them like singular words** to form the possessive. So:
The woman's voice was very quiet. (One woman.)
The women's voices were very quiet. (Two or more women.)
The mouse's nest. The mice's nests.
The child's toy. The children's toys.

RULE 4

When a **proper noun** (i.e. a person's name) ends in -s – like Jones, *James, Charles, Francis, Dickens, Jesus* – you have a choice. You can form the possessive in the regular way: *Jones's, James's, Charles's, Francis's* etc. But spelt like this they produce a lot of hissing. (Try saying, 'Frances's sister'...) The alternative is just to add an apostrophe to the end of the word: *Jones' office, James' friend, Dickens' novels, Jesus' words.*

NOUNS – YOU MUST AGREE

When a noun is the subject of the sentence, it must 'agree' with the verb. This means that if the noun is plural, the verb must be plural too.
The boys were playing. (NOT The boys was playing.)

ERROR ALERT!!
If there are several words in between the subject (noun or pronoun) and its verb, you may forget whether it is singular or plural.
*The pile of dirty clothes lying around the floor **looks** disgusting.*
    (Not *look*; pile is singular)
*The right to elect our leaders and the freedom we have fought so hard to maintain **are** extremely important.*
(Not *is*; right and freedom are *important*. – plural verb needed.)

Certain collective nouns – like *committee, class, team* – may be treated as singular or plural, depending on what the speaker means. So you can say either: *The class has improved this term* or *The class have improved this term* – depending on whether you see the class as a single unit or as a collection of individuals.

PERSONAL PRONOUNS – THEY CAN BE TRICKY

Personal pronouns can appear in four difference 'cases' or functions in a sentence: as subject, as object, to indicate possession, or as a possessive adjective. They change their form according to person, number and 'case'. Here they are, set out as a table.

SINGULAR				PLURAL			
Subject	Object	Possessive	Adjective	Subject	Object	Possessive	Adjective
I	me	mine	my	we	us	ours	our
you	you	yours	your	you	you	yours	your
he	him	his	his	they	them	theirs	their
she	her	hers	her	they	them	theirs	their
it	it	-	its	they	them	theirs	their
who	whom	-	whose	who	whom	-	whose
one	one	-	ones	-	-	-	-

WHO OR WHOM?

Use *who* for the subject or complement:
    Who broke my pencil? My brother, that's who!
Use *whom* when it is the object or indirect object.
    This is Peter, whom I think you have met. He is a man for whom I have the greatest admiration.

WHO OR WHOM?
If you're not sure whether to use who or whom, turn the words around like this: *I think you have met ... him.* (Not, obviously, he;– so this must be the object case – therefore *whom*) *I have the greatest admiration for ... him* (not he; therefore *whom*.)

We use the 'object case' of the pronoun after prepositions: *with me, from him, to her, by them, for us, through whom,* etc.

ERROR ALERT!!
Do you say 'mum and I' or 'mum and me'? It is considered impolite to put yourself first, so **don't** write 'me and my mum'.
    Whether you use *me* or *I* again depends on the 'case'.
    Mum and I went shopping. (Subject.)
    You wouldn't say 'me went shopping' – so *mum and I.*
    The map helped mum and me to find the street. (Object)
    He gave mum and me clear directions. (Indirect object)

ADJECTIVES BY DEGREES

Adjectives are said to have three 'degrees':
> *Mary is **tall**.* (positive degree)
> *Mary is **taller** than Kate.* (comparative degree)
> *Mary is the **tallest** girl in her class.* (superlative degree)

The **comparative** degree is used to compare two things.
> *This is my elder brother.* (Elder than me.)
> *James is the elder of the two.*

The **superlative** degree is used to compare three or more things; it implies that something is superior to all others in the particular quality that the adjective expresses.
> *The youngest sister went to my school.* (Implies there were at least three. If there were only two, I should say, *The younger sister.*)
> *This car is our newest model.* (Superior in 'newness' to all others we have.) *Hugh is the fastest runner in the group.*

Short adjectives form their comparative and superlative degrees by adding -er and -est:
> *late, later, latest; big, bigger, biggest; clever, cleverer, cleverest.*

Longer adjectives use the words more and most instead:
> *fortunate, more fortunate, most fortunate; beautiful, more beautiful, most beautiful; irritating, more irritating, most irritating.*

-ER OR -EST
You should **never** use both *-er* and more, or *-est* and *most*, together. It is incorrect to say:
more cleverer, more taller, most easiest, most biggest.

Some common adjectives form their comparative and superlative degrees in an irregular way:
> *good, better, best; bad, worse, worst; little, less, least; much, more, most; many, more, most; far, farther/ further, farthest/ furthest*

A FEW MEANINGS
The adjective *few* has three slightly different meanings:
A few leaves have fallen. (Means: a small number have fallen.)
Few leaves have fallen. (Means: not many have fallen.)
The few leaves that fell have been swept up. (Means: all those which did fall have been swept.)

ERROR ALERT!!
Only use *few* with 'count nouns' (ones that can be counted). With 'non-count' nouns (quantity not number), use *little, less*. So: *fewer bottles, less milk; fewer pounds, less money.* To say 'less pounds' is incorrect.

NOUNS, PRONOUNS, ADJECTIVES

NOUNS

1. Give the correct **PLURAL FORM** for the following:

baby	....	woman	....
box	....	tomato	....
monkey	....	enemy	....
crisis	....	tooth	....
calf	....	knife	....

2. In the following passage all the **APOSTROPHES** have been left out. Put them in.

Im afraid shes not coming. I knew she wouldnt. I noticed the look on Janes face, you see. Im only upset for the childrens sake. Its little Jamess birthday in two weeks time, and I remember the look on the other lads faces when they saw their mums car outside. Its not womens fault they have to work, of course. But I wish theyd at least get here for their babies birthdays. They should follow Mrs Greens example. She takes a real interest in her daughters welfare.

3. Which of the following **SENTENCES** is incorrect, and why?

a The two kids from the house down the road was having a great time.
b The collection of books Elisabeth left on Saturday have been tidied away.
c The two girls have apologised for what they did, and I think each of them are genuinely sorry.
d The team have really practised hard this season.

PRONOUNS

4. Supply suitable **PRONOUNS** in the blanks in this passage.

There's one person ... I must thank. He is the one ... photo I showed you. ... saved my sister and ...... from drowning. ... would neither of ...... be alive if it wasn't for ...... She and ...... had gone for a walk by .... that morning. My sister had forgotten ...... coat, so ...... was cold, and ...... decided to run to keep ...... warm. ...... fell down the bank, and ...... came tumbling after .... Luckily, ... heard ...... cries for help, and came to ...... rescue.

COMPARATIVE ADJECTIVES

5. Correct the mistakes in the following sentences.

John is the slowest of the two, but he make less mistakes. And he's more friendlier than his brother. I'd say he's one of the peacefullest people I know.

Answers on page 126.

INTRODUCTION

Here you will learn how words are grouped together to form phrases, clauses and sentences. This part of grammar is called syntax, meaning, in Greek, 'the orderly arrangement of parts'.

PHRASES

A PHRASE IS A GROUP OF WORDS MAKING INCOMPLETE SENSE.

It does not contain a finite verb. There are several different kinds.

• A **prepositional phrase** is a group of words introduced by a preposition:

> *on the street, under the piano, above your head*

• A **participial phrase** is a group of words introduced by a participle:

> *making a fuss; living like a lord; being a nuisance* (present participles)
> *torn to pieces; spoken in jest; told by an idiot* (past participles)

• An **infinitive phrase** is a group of words introduced by an infinitive verb

> *to try his luck; to play the game; to shout for joy; to have won the war*

A phrase may do the work of an adjective, an adverb or a noun:

Adjectival phrases:

> The wreck *at the bottom of the ocean*. The man *waving a red flag*. The girl *with the beautiful smile*.

Adverbial phrases:

> He wrote it *with great care*. I found this *under my bed*. They will see you *in the morning*.

Noun phrases:

These perform all the same functions as Parts of Sentence that single nouns do.

Noun phrases acting as subject:

> *Climbing mountains* can be dangerous.
> *To explain my story* seemed impossible.

Noun phrases acting as object:

> I enjoy *quietly reading a book*. Please remember *to put the kettle on*.

Noun phrases acting as complement:

> My favourite hobby is *making jam*.
> His next action was *to phone the police*.

PHRASES

1. Identify the **PREPOSITIONAL, PARTICIPIAL** and **INFINITIVE PHRASES** in the following passage. (Write them out as 3 lists.)

> After about an hour, I found Julian by the swimming pool. He was sitting under an umbrella with a drink on the table in front of him. He seemed to have forgotten the others. Torn between concern for Mary and wanting to teach him a lesson, I decided to speak my mind. Summoning up my courage, I told him what I thought. He, on the other hand, appeared to take no notice. Diving into the water, he disappeared for a while, swimming under water and coming up for air at the other end of the pool. Distracted by this performance, and annoyed at his behaviour, I did not notice Mary walking towards me.

2. In the following sentences, identify whether the phrases in italics are **ADJECTIVAL, ADVERBIAL** or **NOUN PHRASES**.

> **a** The house *at the end of our road* was built *in the eighteenth century*. An old woman lives there *with her dog*.
> **b** My maths teacher likes *to speak very fast*. *Keeping track* can be difficult
> **c** The document, *torn to shreds*, was discovered *lying on the ground — underneath a pile of books*

3. In the following passage, find one **ADJECTIVAL PHRASE**, one **ADVERBIAL PHRASE** and two **NOUN PHRASES**.

> This is a matter of the utmost urgency, and you must carry out my instructions with all possible speed. Wasting time now will certainly mean us all getting killed.

Answers on page 127.

Don't cheat! Only look them up when you have finished the exercise.

CLAUSES

A CLAUSE IS A GROUP OF WORDS WHICH CONTAINS A FINITE VERB.

There are two basic types:

The **main clause** is the 'backbone' of the sentence – the main statement. It may stand on its own as a simple sentence.

> *The stranger spoke*

The **dependent clause** (or subordinate clause), like the phrase, may act as an adjective, an adverb or a noun. It is said to 'depend' on the main clause, or be subordinate to it.

> The stranger, *whom nobody had noticed*, spoke.

SIMPLE, COMPOUND AND COMPLEX SENTENCES

A **simple sentence** contains only one finite verb. It expresses a single idea, and it consists of one main clause.

> *Harry trains elephants*

This can be built up as elaborately as you like with the addition of adjectives, adverbs or any of the different kinds of phrases that you looked at on page .....

> *Amazing young Harry in his spare time expertly trains even stubborn elephants.*

But as long as it has only one finite verb *(trains)*, it is still a **simple sentence**.

A **compound** sentence contains two or more main clauses, each with a finite verb, joined by a co-ordinating conjunction (*and, but, or*).

> *Harry trains elephants, but Bob prefers monkeys.*

In these sentences both clauses have equal weight. They are both main clauses. Sometimes clauses linked like this are called **co-ordinating clauses**.

A **complex sentence** is one which contains a main clause and one or more dependent clauses.

> *When he finds the time, Harry, who is an unusual person, trains elephants, which he loves because they are such intelligent creatures.*

We still have our basic main clause – *Harry trains elephants* – but now we have **four dependent clauses**.

TYPES OF DEPENDENT CLAUSE
ADJECTIVE CLAUSES

The man, *who was wearing a dark blue coat*, seemed nervous.
I returned to my work, *which was nearly finished*.

Adjective clauses are normally introduced by a relative pronoun (*who, which, that, whose, whom*), but it often happens that the relative pronoun is understood, not expressed.

The girl *I wanted to meet* was not there. (Means 'the girl who I wanted to meet')
I left the work *I had been trying to finish*. (Means 'the work that I had been trying to finish')

ADVERB CLAUSES There are several kinds:

- **Adverb clause of time** (when?)
  While he was talking, the dog escaped. He didn't notice *until it was too late*.

- **Adverb clause of place** (where?)
  Please sit where you *like*. *Wherever I go*, I find people like you.

- **Adverb clause of manner** (how?)
  He did his work *as well as he could*. It was all arranged *as she would have wanted*. It did not turn out *as you might expect*.

- **Adverb clause of comparison** (compared to what?)
  This is going to be harderthan you *think*.
  This car is better than the one I used to *own*.

- **Adverb clause of degree** (to what extent?)
  John is not as daft *as you seem to imagine*. He ate *as many as he possibly could*.

- **Adverb clause of reason** (why?)
  Since you have done no revision, you will probably fail your exam. I decided to go home, *because it was getting late*.

- **Adverb clause of purpose** (for what purpose?)
  The teacher explained the method *so that everyone could understand.*
  In order that we can get the matter cleared up, will everyone please listen to Inspector Brown.

- **Adverb clause of result** (with what result?)
  He laughed so much *that he nearly choked*. People continued to pour in, *so that the room was soon overcrowded*.

- **Adverb clause of condition** (on what condition?)

  If you come to my office, I will give you the key. *Provided he tells the truth*, he will not get into trouble. *Unless we stop this now*, the situation could become serious.

- **Adverb clause of concession** (in spite of what?)

  Although I have never met her, I feel as if I know her. *Though he tried every week*, he never won the lottery. *Even if you paid me*, I wouldn't see that film.

- **Noun clauses.** These may be:

the **subject** of the main verb:

  How you could do such a thing is something I shall never know.

the **object** of the main verb:

  I do not believe *that he is guilty*.

the **complement** of a verb of being or becoming:

  This is *what she saw*.

in **apposition** to (i.e. positioned next to) a noun or pronoun:

  Peter Jackson, *radio journalist*, was hurt in the explosion

placed after a **preposition**:

  He gave an account of *what had happened*.

DON'T GET LOST!

It is important when you are constructing your sentences not to lose sight of your main clause. It forms the 'backbone' of the sentence. When you are dealing with long, complex sentences, it is useful to analyse your sentence, breaking it down into its separate clauses. Start by identifying your main clause. Then see how many dependent clauses there are (count the finite verbs!). Finally, try to work out their functions. Here is an example for you:

Because I was in a hurry that morning, **I failed to notice** that Mary, who liked to arrive early whenever she could, had not turned up, even though it was pay day.

1. Adverb clause of reason – *because I was in a hurry that morning.*
2. Main clause – *I failed to notice.*
3. Noun clause, – *that Mary had not turned up.* Object of 'notice'.
4. Adjective clause -*who generally liked to arrive early.* Qualifies 'Mary'.
5. Adverb clause of time – *whenever she could.* Modifies 'liked'.
6. Adverb clause of concession – *even though it was pay day.*

CLAUSES

1. Underline the **MAIN CLAUSES** in the following passage:

> If James, who is really quite bright, does not learn to work, he will never, in spite of his talents, be much of a success. His parents, who are very proud of him, will be very disappointed. When he does work, he can, if he chooses, be one of the best in the class.

2. One of these sentences is **COMPOUND** and the other is **COMPLEX**. Which is which?

> **a** He was very young and had had little experience, but nonetheless I trusted him.
>
> **b** He was the kind of man who would remain calm in a crisis.

3. Underline the **ADJECTIVE CLAUSES** in the following passage:

> My dog George, who is one of the daftest animals that ever lived, likes to be taken for his daily walk on the common which lies just across the road from our house. Last Tuesday there was a woman whom I hadn't seen before out walking with another dog, to which for reasons of his own George took an instant dislike. It had a long, gleaming coat its owner must have spent ages grooming, and a general air of superiority that obviously got up George's soft black nose. He decided to attack. The woman whose dog it was let out a scream that could have been heard three miles away.

4. Underline the **ADVERB CLAUSES** in the following. See if you can identify the type (time, place, manner, comparison, degree, reason, purpose, result, condition, concession) of each one.

> I grabbed hold of George and held him as tightly as I could. And then, because I was feeling embarrassed, and so that the woman would think I was taking the matter seriously – even if I wasn't – I gave him a tremendous smack which made him yelp. The other dog, who was quite unhurt and behaving as though nothing had happened, looked on with a smug expression. The woman, however, kept shouting that if she ever saw me or my dog again she would send for the police. I stood where I was and tried hard to look sorrier than I really felt. Although I was cross with George, I did feel she was overdoing it a bit. Such a fuss she made that even the dog began to look somewhat ashamed while all this was going on. Finally, after George and I got away, I told him he was a bad dog who behaved so badly whenever I took him out that he didn't deserve to go walkies with his nice kind master. He didn't look particularly impressed.

CLAUSES continued

5. The following passage contains a number of **NOUN CLAUSES** (that is, clauses doing the work of a noun). Can you identify them, and say what part they are playing (subject, object, complement, in apposition, following a preposition) in the sentence?

> This is exactly what I had hoped for. The fact that we have caught this man at last is a great relief. Of course we know nothing about what happened before yesterday. How he came to be in that house is something we shall probably never find out. But that he knew what he was doing is beyond doubt. I haven't decided yet what I shall tell HQ; I'll think about that when I have time. Meanwhile, I think we all deserve a drink.

6. Analyse the following sentences, breaking each one down into its separate clauses. List the clauses, and try to identify the function of each one in the sentence. (Remember that in a compound sentence there is more than one main clause.)

> **a** Even though I like New York, which is after all where I was born, I avoid going there if I can help it, because whenever I am there, I'm afraid that I might bump into Harry.
> **b** After they had finished lunch, Joel, who had certainly had too much to drink, clumsily escorted Alison, who hadn't said a word all through lunch, into the garden, where he promptly proposed to her.
> **c** Once the exam was over, Hugh decided that, since he had probably failed, it might be best if he slipped away unnoticed, so he collected the books he had borrowed, as he would have no further need of them, and left as quietly as he could.

Answers on page 127.

Don't cheat! Only look them up when you have finished the exercise.

INTRODUCTION

In everything you write, there is (or should be!) a thread running through – a thread of logic and order. Any sentence, from the simplest and most basic to the longest, most complex one you can think of, will have a clear structure. Your sentences must always be constructed in such a way that your reader can follow the thread of your argument.

PARAGRAPHS

The same thing applies when it comes to grouping your sentences into paragraphs. But first, let's agree what we mean by a paragraph.

A **paragraph** is a group of one or more sentences on a **single theme or topic**, forming a **distinct section** of a piece of writing, and **beginning on a new line**.

When you set out to write something, what you are doing is setting down a series of **ideas**. But it's no good just throwing your ideas at the page in any old order. You have to group them in a coherent way, so that they follow on logically from each other. For each main idea, you need a separate paragraph.

HELP YOUR READER

Glance down any page and you can tell at once when a new paragraph begins. This helps you as a reader, because you know that the writer is moving onto a new aspect of the story or subject. This is how your reader keeps track of your line of thought.

DON'T BE A WOOLLY THINKER!
One of the most common errors in writing is failing to organise paragraphs properly. This means that there is no proper logical structure to the writing. And that means that the person isn't thinking clearly. If your thinking is woolly and confused, you will confuse your reader. So **never lose sight of the thread.**

A PARAGRAPH FOR EACH TOPIC

You will find that your ideas on any subject fall naturally into distinct **topics** or **themes**. For example, suppose you are writing a piece on, say, keeping pets. You might want to sort your ideas into different piles – 'Cats', 'Dogs', 'Gerbils and Hamsters', 'Tortoises' – and put all that you had to say on each topic together. (It wouldn't be very helpful if, for instance, in the middle of talking about how to groom your cat, you suddenly switched to saying what to feed to your tortoise. And in fact you would probably want to make further sub-groups for 'feeding', 'grooming', 'exercise' etc.) Each topic needs to have a paragraph to itself.

TOPIC SENTENCE

Look at any piece of writing. You will find that nearly all paragraphs contain a **topic sentence** which expresses the main idea of that paragraph. This commonly comes at the beginning of the paragraph:

> *'Greece has a long and fascinating history...'*
> *'Nuclear power is an efficient way of generating electricity...'*
> *'Jonathan had always wanted to fly an aeroplane...'*

The topic sentence signals to the reader that this paragraph will be about Greece/nuclear power/Jonathan and flying, or whatever it might be.

CHECKPOINT: SUMMARISE YOUR PARAGRAPHS

Take a look at a piece of your own writing. If you have constructed it properly, it should be possible to give a brief, one-line summary of each paragraph. And those paragraph summaries in turn should give you a summary of the whole piece. If you can't summarise a paragraph because it deals with more than one topic, divide it up further into as many paragraphs as it needs.

TYPES OF PARAGRAPH

Paragraphs which **begin with the topic sentence** (as in the examples above) are called **loose paragraphs**. This type is by far the most common.

Another way to construct a paragraph is to put the **topic sentence at the end**. Paragraphs like this are called **periodic paragraphs**. This kind of construction is often used for dramatic effect:

> *'It turned out that Harry had left two days previously. The taxi driver had been lying to me, and now I had missed my chance. It was a disaster.'*

A third type of paragraph contains the topic sentence in the middle. The opening sentence prepares for the introduction of the theme, and there is a rounding off at the end.

> *'I should like to make one thing clear. Anyone who fails this test will have to repeat it. So make sure you revise properly.'*

GIVE YOUR WORK A COHERENT STRUCTURE

If you are telling a story, you will probably organise your material in **chronological order**. Sometimes, however, you might want to use the device known as 'flashback' to write about events in a different sequence.

In all other kinds of writing, you will need to consider what is the best and **most logical order** to present your ideas. Which sequence will make it easiest for your reader? This is especially important when you are presenting an argument. You need to build up your 'case' logically, step by step, so that your reader can follow the argument and then (you hope) accept your conclusion.

STRUCTURE EACH PARAGRAPH COHERENTLY

Not only does each paragraph need to be coherent within itself: the writing also needs to be coherent as a whole. This is achieved by **linking your ideas**. Within the paragraph, each sentence should follow on logically from the last one. Consider this paragraph.

> *'We cannot really give an answer to this question. This is because we have not been given sufficient information. Although the government has released certain details about the situation, there are still many gaps in our knowledge. So we can at best only hazard a guess at the answer.'*

Sentence 1 makes a statement. Sentence two gives a reason why – *because*. Sentence 3 elaborates on the reason – *although… still*. Sentence 4 draws a conclusion – **so**

ALWAYS CHECK THAT YOUR PARAGAPH IS COHERENT.

LINK YOUR PARAGRAPHS COHERENTLY

In the same way that you link your sentences, you need to link paragraphs so that the whole piece is coherent. These are many ways to do this. Here are a few useful linking phrases:

> *First of all, secondly, in addition, finally;*
> *in the same way, similarly, again;*
> *on the other other hand, in contrast, however;*
> *immediately, at once, soon, next day, after a while, a year later;*
> *near, opposite, below, in front of, at a distance, further off;*
> *for instance, for example, such as;*
> *so, hence, accordingly, thus, to conclude.*

ALWAYS CHECK THAT YOUR WORK IS COHERENTLY STRUCTURED.

PARAGRAPHS

Divide the following story into 6 or 7 paragraphs. Give each paragraph a title. Identify the linking phrases used by the writer.

The countryside flew past, but I hardly saw it. I couldn't stop thinking about the sister I was going to meet. My very own twin sister! What would she be like? What would she feel about me? Had she been pleased to discover that I existed? My mind went back to the moment, just over a month ago, when I had received the letter. It had lain untouched for two days on the hall table in my Paris flat before I opened it. I had thought it was just another bill. As I ripped open the envelope I took in at a glance that it came from my solicitor. I sat down to read it. As my eyes ran down the page, a flood of violent emotions ran through me. Shock first, then wild excitement. The thought of this unknown sister thrilled me, and I cried out like a madman. But then came anger. Why had no-one ever told us that somewhere we had a twin? Suddenly my whole life was laid before me. At last I understood that aching sense. I had always felt there was something missing. A gaping hole in my very being. And now, perhaps, that missing part of myself was going to be restored to me. I continued to stare out of the window. I began to notice how the country through which the train was passing was becoming more hilly. We were getting closer. Not very long to wait now. Yet, oh, how unbearable the waiting seemed! After a while I became aware that the man sitting opposite me had been watching me intently for quite a long time. He seemed to be very interested in me. Could he read my thoughts, I wondered? I had no-one to confide in over all this business. Perhaps it might be a relief to talk to someone. Why not this stranger? I decided then and there to tell him everything.

Note: Feel free to write the rest of the story yourself. It is, of course, the other half of the story begun on page 99. It doesn't have an ending, so you can take it wherever you like!

Suggested answers on page 128.

Don't cheat! Only look them up when you have finished the exercise.

FULL STOPS are needed

- at the end of every sentence
- to indicate an abbreviation
- to mark a breaking off – *what on earth...*
- to show that some words have been missed out.
  Read the passage 'When he began ... she was dead.'

QUESTION MARKS AND EXCLAMATION MARKS are needed

- surprise, surprise! – after questions and exclamations:
  What did you say? Good grief!

CAPITAL LETTERS are needed

- at the beginning of every sentence;
- at the beginning of a piece of direct speech
  Clara looked up and said, 'Fancy that!'
- for proper nouns: *Monday, January, Italy, Paris, William Tell*
- for the main words of all titles: *Prime Minister, Prince of Wales, The Independent, The House at Pooh Corner; Marks and Spencer*
- at the beginning of each new line of poetry
  (though some modern poets prefer not to follow this convention).

COMMAS are needed

- to separate words, phrases or clauses in a list.
  She bought bread, eggs, apples and chocolate.
  Go down the road, round the corner, and into the park.
  > **Tip:** the comma before *and* is optional before a phrase.
  > *He took the gun, inspected it carefully, aimed it at his wife, and fired.*

- to separate consecutive adjectives where the comma is like *and*
  big, juicy, ripe apples (You might say *big and juicy and ripe*.)
  > **Tip:** where the final adjective and the noun taken together express a single idea, you don't put a comma between them and the preceding adjective: *poor little boy; fresh brown bread.* (You wouldn't say *poor and little boy*, or *fresh and brown bread*.)

- to separate two or more sentences which are linked by and or but.
  I have never travelled by air, and I don't intend to start now.
  You may say what you like, but you will not persuade me.
- to separate off introductory words, phrases or clauses.
  To be honest, I don't care.
  Actually, I have already read that book.

- to separate 'sentence adverbs' from the rest of the sentence:
  Mr Simmonds, however, was of a different opinion.
  Unfortunately, you have given me the wrong address.
  > **Tip:** when *however* is used to mean 'no matter how' **no** comma is required following it: *She was determined to wait, however long it might take.*

- before 'tagging on' clauses:
  You do believe me, don't you? It's a waste of time, isn't it?
- to mark off the person being addressed:
  Please come in, John. Hurry up, you idiot, or we'll be late!
- before and after a word or phrase in apposition:
  I need a map, a really up-to-date one, to take with me.
- to mark off words like *yes, no, thank you, well, please.*
  No, I never drink coffee, thank you. Yes, it is odd. Give it to me, please.
- as a kind of brackets, to mark off an inserted thought:
  Barnaby, as I think I told you, is a talented actor.
- to mark off a participial phrase:
  Having got this far, they were reluctant to turn back.
- to mark off adverbial clauses, especially when they start the sentence:
  If you say that again, I shall scream.
- to mark off an adjective clause which merely comments but does not limit or define:
  The apples, which are mouldy, should be thrown away.
  > (i.e. all the apples) **but**

  The apples which are mouldy should be thrown away.
  > (i.e. only those apples which are mouldy)

NEVER PUT A COMMA BETWEEN TWO SENTENCES

Instead you can put either a full stop:
He tried to stop her. She was too quick for him.
or a comma followed by a conjunction such as *and* or *but.*
He tried to stop her, but she was too quick for him.
or, if you want to link your two sentences more closely than you would with a full stop, you can use a semi-colon:
He tried to stop her; she was too quick for him.
But **NEVER** write:
He tried to stop her, she was too quick for him.
This is what is known as a 'run-on' sentence. There are two subjects, and two verbs: *he* tried and *she* was. So there are two sentences, and to put a comma between them is incorrect.

APOSTROPHES are used:

- to indicate **possession**:
  the lady's hat, the ladies' hats, a week's holiday, men's trousers.
  (To remind yourself of the rules about using apostrophes for possessive adjectives, see pages 103-107.

• to indicate **contraction** (i.e. you've left some letters out…):
'flu, (influenza) *'cause, ma'am, fo'c'sle* (forecastle)
don't, didn't, won't, isn't, aren't, I'll, he'll, you'll; you're (you are), *we're,*
they're (they are); *it's* (it is or it has).

WHEN NOT TO USE APOSTROPHES
The apostrophe is **not** used for possessive pronouns *yours, ours, hers, its* or *theirs*. It **is**, however, used for *one's*.
One creates one's own fate. Life must take its course.
• It's a very common mistake, which finds its way into many people's writing, to spell the possessive pronoun its, 'it's' – which of course means 'it is'!

• *'its',* meaning 'belonging to it' does **not** have an apostrophe
I've, you've, I'm, he's, she's; you'd (you would or you had), *I'd, he'd, she'd, we'd, they'd; I'd've* (I would have)

NEVER write 'I would of' say, I would/should/could/might HAVE.

PUNCTUATION OF DIRECT SPEECH

• Begin a new paragraph every time the speaker changes.
• Enclose the words spoken, and the accompanying punctuation, in inverted commas. (NB: The punctuation, whether comma, exclamation mark or full stop, must come **inside** the inverted commas.
"What is going on?" I asked. "I don't understand."
• The spoken words are followed by a comma, not a full stop, when the verb of saying comes afterwards. (If the spoken words are a question, use a question mark.)
"Well, it's hard to explain," she replied.
• When the subject and verb of saying come before the spoken words, they are followed by a comma, and the first word of the speech has a capital letter.
He said, "All the same, please do your best."
• When the spoken sentence is interrupted, with the verb of saying in the middle of it, put a comma and inverted commas at the end of the first part of the speech, then the subject and verb of saying, then another comma before opening inverted commas for the speech to continue. The next word of the spoken sentence has a small letter, because it is a continuation of the sentence.
"Why didn't you tell me," she said, "that you felt like this?"

QUOTATION MARKS are also used

- when you quote someone's words (for example in a report):
  The Prime Minister said that the situation was "entirely under control", and people should feel safe to return to their homes and "live normally".
- when you are quoting from a book: (In this case the part in quotation marks is referred to as a 'quotation', not a 'quote'.)
  Othello's speech begins with the words, "Put out the light, and then put out the light.".
  Notice that the commas and full stops come *outside* the quotation marks.
- for the title of a poem or song, a chapter of a book or an article in a magazine: (Usually single quotation marks are used for this.)
  Matthew Arnold's poem 'Dover Beach' was published in 1867.
  Chapter 6, 'The Court of Queen Elizabeth', is particularly interesting.

THE BOOK OR THE PERSON?
It is not incorrect to put the titles of whole works – novels, plays, films and television programmes – in quotation marks, but it is the accepted practice to put them in *italics* (or <u>underline</u> them in handwritten text). Where the title is also the name of one of the characters, this makes it clear whether we are speaking of the book or the person.

- to indicate foreign words:
  She has a certain 'joie de vivre' which is quite out of keeping with the current 'zeitgeist'.
  > **Tip:** You can also use italics (or underlining if you're writing by hand) instead of quotation marks in this kind of situation:
  > *She has a certain joie de vivre which is quite out of keeping with the current zeitgeist.*

- to enclose a word or words that are being explained or translated.
  The word 'zeitgeist' means 'spirit of the age'. It comes from German 'Zeit', meaning 'time' and 'Geist', which is similar to English 'ghost' and means 'spirit'.
- when you want to show that a word or words are being used sarcastically or with a special meaning.
  Jonathan was being 'clever' as usual.

DASHES are used

in **pairs** when breaking off a sentence
- to insert an afterthought:
  I don't know whether you realised – I had better explain myself properly – but my mother belonged to the Devonshire family.
- to add an explanatory comment:
  We shall be studying Epistemology – that's what philosophers call the theory of knowledge – as part of the course.
- to insert a short list:
  The whole family – aunts, uncles, cousins, grandparents, children – were gathered for the wedding.

SINGLY

- when breaking off a sentence for an abrupt change of thought or to add on a related remark:
  I think his wife ended up in Paris — but that's another story.
  The flowers you sent were gorgeous — I've always loved lilies.
- to emphasise a repeated word:
  This is going to cost a lot of money — money we don't have.
- to bring together a number of items:
  Families with children, old people, students, the sick — all these will get extra financial help.

BRACKETS (always two) are used like dashes

- for 'asides' and for enclosing additional information:
  The house at the end of the road (which used to belong to my uncle) is going to be demolished.

  Tip: If there is a bracketed **phrase** at the end of a sentence, the full stop comes after the bracket; but if the whole sentence is enclosed in brackets, the full stop comes inside them.
  Please be quiet (for just a few minutes). But -
  They find it impossible to be quiet. (They're too excited.)

PARENTHESIS

You can also use pairs of commas in much the same way as brackets or dashes, to mark off an inserted thought.

This device — of putting extra information in between commas, dashes or brackets — is called **parenthesis**. Use it to keep your reader focused on the main thread of what you are saying. The reader's mind takes note of the part in parenthesis, but quite easily and naturally jumps over it to continue following what came before it.

The reader's mind (which naturally focuses on one thing at a time) can be directed — without him or her necessarily noticing the fact — exactly where you wish it to be.

SEMI-COLONS are used:

to separate clauses which could stand on their own but which are closely related, especially when
- the second clause expands or explains the first one:
  I wasn't exactly afraid; I was just worried for your sake.
- the clauses describe a sequence of actions:
  The pair burst into the shop; they forced the owner to open the till; then they grabbed the money and ran.
- the clauses describe different aspects of the same topic:
  The old house was full of strange noises tonight; the wind howled in the chimney; doors and windows rattled; rain lashed against the windows.

- you want to suggest a contrast:
  Most of my family love winter sports; I hate them.
  In youth he was full of idealistic fervour; now in old age he had lost all interest.
- the clause begins with an explanatory phrase such as
  even so, therefore, for example, nevertheless, however.
  He was always so kind; for example, he lent us his house.
  There's not much hope; nevertheless, we must at least try.
  Most of his books had gone; however, he did find this one.

  > **Tip:** Notice that a comma is normally required after *however*. This does **not** apply, however, when it is used to mean 'no matter how':
  > *He couldn't make her hear, however hard he shouted.*

- to mark off a series of phrases or clauses which themselves contain commas:
  Scattered about the room there were papers, books, magazines, personal letters; various items of clothing, including the sweat-shirt he had been wearing the night I had seen him, a pair of socks, some trainers, and an old jacket; several discarded bottles, an ashtray with its contents spilling out onto the floor, a number dirty glasses and plates, one of which had the remains of a meal still sticking to it; a pile of videotapes, none of them particularly interesting; and, lying in a corner, mercifully undamaged, his precious violin.

COLONS are used:

- to introduce a list, especially after the words 'as follows' or 'the following':
  The following people have gained A grades: Simon Barnes, Jenny Cartwright, Sally Ford, Jeremy North
- to introduce a long quotation or speech:
  Henry V addresses his troops before the battle: "This day is called the feast of Crispian…"
- before a clause which explains the previous statement. (The colon has the force of 'that is' or 'namely'.)
  I want only one thing: that you should be happy.
- to express a strong contrast:
  Most of the army turned to flee: one man stood firm.
- to introduce a climax or concluding clause:
  Now that his ordeal was over and he could at last to think clearly, he was able to come to a decision: he would return to Kandahar.
- to make a pointed connection:
  Although Laura did not fully admit even to herself what were her motives, it would not have taken a cynical observer long to work out why she was making such an effort to attract this particular young man: his father just happened to own one of the largest banking firms in the country.

STRUCTURE OF LANGUAGE

PARTS OF SPEECH (Page 81)
1. <u>Nouns</u>: window, car, Cambridge Road, time, month, James, heart, degree, hope.
2. <u>Verbs</u>: had left, threw, began, to think, had been, was expecting, to go, was, could, have acted, wondered, had been given, to think, would laugh, heard, said, will, seem.
3. <u>Pronouns</u>: she, herself, and, who, her, nobody, it, who, everyone, they, themselves, it, everyone, their, anyone, he, her, she, him.
4. <u>Adjectives</u>: small, her, heavy, long, steep, young, alone, strange, unfriendly, first, that, hot, few, two, three, few, grim.
5. <u>Adverbs</u>: stupidly, yesterday, probably, there, very, nearly, away, fortunately, however, hastily, before, now, perhaps, really, quickly.
6. <u>Conjunctions</u>: if, but, as, unless, before, neither, nor, although, because, and.
7. <u>Prepositions</u>: across, on, under, on, beside, from, out of, into, up, towards.

PARTS OF SENTENCE. (Page 90)
(NOTE: Where the main word is accompanied by adjuncts, it is given in bold type.)
1. <u>Subject</u>: door, a shabbily dressed old **man**; He; I; I; This; street; thin, hungry-looking **children**.
2. <u>Object</u>: corner; keys; front **door;** my **luck**; him; chance; bell.
3. <u>Indirect Object</u>: me; her; the girl; **someone** behind the door; me; the hidden **person**; me.
4. <u>Complement</u>: surprisingly **beautiful**; frightened; ashamed; ridiculous; outof hand; much **worse**; very **angry**; **white** with fury; ominously **silent**.

VERB FORMS (Page 95)
1. <u>Verbs</u>: was (status), had (action), met (action) were studying (action), seemed (status), could have guessed (action) was (status), can't believe (action) has happened (action).
2. <u>Auxiliary verbs</u>: should/would, were, have, shall/will, had, am, have been.
3. a We were very pleased to hear that our cars were ready, and we will collect them this afternoon.
3. b The girl says she saw the man helping himself, but she does not think the man realised he was being watched.
4. a His name is Peter, and he is here to talk about himself and the book he has written.
   b (i) I am so happy, I hardly know what do with myself. **(ii)** You are so happy, you hardly know what to do with yourself.
5. a imperative; **b** interrogative; **c** indicative; **d** subjunctive
6. a passive; **b** active

VERB TENSES (Page 99)
(NOTE: Numbers refer to paragraphs.)

1. stared (past); had been watching (past perfect continuous); interest (present); was (past); had decided (past perfect); would say (future in past); spoke (past); know (present); are wondering (present continuous); said (past); found (past); will tell (future).

2. was(n't) meaning (past continuous); stammered (past).

3. Do(n't) worry (present imperative form); said (past); am going (present continuous); am (present); were separated (past – passive form); see (present); have been living (perfect continuous); have never met (perfect); will have been (future perfect); did(n't) know (past); existed (past); stopped (past); shook (past); found (past); seems (present); said (past); will meet (future); had told (past perfect); would find (future in past); would be travelling (future in past continuous); would have said (future in past); were (past).

4. said (past); will have been thinking (future perfect continuous); wonder (present); is feeling (present continuous).

5. have thought (perfect); said (past); hope (present); will come (future); want (present); meet (present); do(n't) know (present); will have told (future perfect); do(n't) know (present); will react (future).

6. was watching (past continuous); had fallen (past perfect); began (past); could (past).

7. interrupted (past); knew (past); gave (past); were born (past – passive form); turned (past); am hoping (present continuous); can trace (present); am (present); will have come (future perfect).

8. fell (past); turned (past); said (past); ca(n't) explain (present); feels (present); have been living (perfect continuous); will have been thinking (future perfect continuous); were (past); are (present); thought (past); were (past); can understand (present).

9. nodded (past); understood (past).

NON-FINITE VERBS (Page 102)

1. finding, found, found; thinking, thought, thought; doing, did, done; weaving, wove, woven; cutting, cut, cut; ringing, rang, rung; taking, took, taken, buying, bought, bought, seeing, saw, seen.

2. <u>Participles</u>: waiting (child), broken (doll); frozen (she); wondering (Alice); smiling (she), expected (response); worn (face); backing (child), edging (child); fearing (Alice), wandering (girl), grabbing (Alice) lifting (Alice); fighting (child); terrified (she).

3. <u>Infinitives</u>: to act, to put, to beging, to wait, to go.
  <u>Verbal Nouns</u>: talking, training, fighting, understanding, being, knowing.

NOUNS, PRONOUNS, ADJECTIVES (Page 107)

1. babies, boxes, monkeys, crises, calves, women, tomatoes, enemies, teeth, knives.

2. I'm, she's, wouldn't, Jane's, I'm. children's, it's, James's (or James') weeks', lads', mum's, women's, they'd, babies', Green's, daughter's.

3. a The two kids were have a great time. (Kids is plural.)
  b The collection of books has been tidied away. (Collection is singular.)
  c I think each of them is genuinely sorry. (Each is singular.)
  d Correct. (Team can be plural if considered as a collection of individuals.)

4. whom, whose, he, me, we, us, him, I, ourselves, her, it, we, ourselves, she (or I), I (or she) her (or me), he, our, our.

5. John is the slower of the two, but he makes fewer mistakes, and he's friendlier (or more friendly) than his brother. I'd say he's one of the most peaceful people I know.

ANSWERS

PHRASES (Page 109)

1. <u>Prepositional phrases</u>: after about an hour, by the swimming pool, under an umbrellia, with a drink, on the table, in front o him, between concern, for Mary, on the other hand, for a while, unmder water, for air, at the other end, of the pool, by this performance, at his behaviour, towards me.

<u>Participial phrases</u>: sitting under an umbrella, torn between concern, wanting to teach him, summoning up my courage, diving into the water, swimming under water, coming up for air, distracted by this performance, annoyed at his behaviour, walking towards me.

<u>Infinitive phrases</u>: to have forgotten, to teach him, to speak my mind, to take no notice.

2. a adjectiveal, adverbial.

  b noun (object), noun (subject)

  c adjectival, adverbial, adverbial

3. of the utmost urgency (adjectival); with al possible speed ()adverbial); wasting time now (noun), us all getting killed (noun)

CLAUSES (Page 113)

1. <u>Main clauses</u>: He will never be much of a success. His parents will be very disappointed. He can be one of the best in the class.

2. a compound **b** complex

3. <u>Adjective clauses</u>: who is one of the daftest animals that ever lived; which lies just across the road; whom I hadn't seen before; to which for reasons of his own George took an instant dislike; its owner must have spent ages grooming; that obviously got up George's soft black nose; whose dog it was; that could have been heard three miles away.

4. <u>Adverb clauses</u>: as tightly as I could (manner); because I was feeling embarrassed (reason); so that the woman would think (purpose); even if I wasn't (concession); as though nothing had happened (manner); if she ever saw me or my dog again (condition); where I was (place); than I really felt (comparison); Although I was cross with George (concession); while all this was going on (time); after George and I got away (time); whenever I took him out (time).

5. <u>Noun clauses</u>: what I had hoped for (complement); that we have caught this man at last (apposition); what happened before yesterday (follows preposition); how he came to be in that house (subject); but that he knew what he was doing (subject); what I shall tell HQ (object); we all deserve a drink (object).

6. a

Even though I like New York	- dependent adverb clause of concession
which is after all where I was born	- dependent adjective clause, describes New York
where I was born,	- dependent adverb clause, complement of is
I avoid going there	- Main clause
if I can help it,	- dependent conditional clause
because I'm afraid	- dependent adverb clause of reason
whenever I am there	- dependent adverb clause of time
that I might bump into Harry	- dependent noun clause, object of I'm afraid

b

After they had finished lunch	- dependent adverb clause of time
Joel clumsily escorted Alison into the garden	– Main clause
who had certainly had too much to drink	- dependent adjective clause, describes Joel
who hadn't said a word all through lunch	- dependent adjective clause, describes Alison
where he promptly proposed to her	- dependent adverb clause of place

c

Once the exam was over	- dependent adverb clause of time
Hugh decided	- Main clause
that it might be best	- dependent noun clause, object of decided
since he had probably failed	- dependent adverb clause of reason
if he slipped away unnoticed	- dependent conditional clause
so he collected the books	- Main (co-ordinating) clause
he had borrowed	- adjective clause (that understood), describes books
as he would have no further need of them	– dependent adverb clause of reason
and left as quietly as he could	- Main (co-ordinating) clause

PARAGRAPHS (Page 118)
(NOTE: These are suggestions. You could break the story down in several ways.)
1. The countryside flew past...
2. My mind went back...
3. As my eyes ran down the page...
4. Suddenly, my whole life...
5. I continued to stare out of the window...
6. After a while...
7. I decided then and there...